MORE

Alternative Shakespeare Auditions for Women

Simon Dunmore

A & C Black • London
Theatre Arts Books / Routledge • New York

First published 2000
by A & C Black (Publishers) Limited
35 Bedford Row, London WC1R 4JH

© 2000 Simon Dunmore

ISBN 0-7136-5277-2

A CIP catalogue record for this book is available from
the British Library.

Published in the USA in 2000 by
Theatre Arts Books / Routledge
29 West 35 Street, New York NY10001

ISBN 0-87830-113-5

CIP catalog record available at the
Library of Congress.

Cover photograph: Nigel Norrington / Arena Images

Typeset in Palatino
Printed and bound in Great Britain by
Creative Print and Design (Wales), Ebbw Vale

Contents

Introduction

Shakespeare is demanded for audition a lot of the time. Unfortunately for auditioners, auditionees tend to choose from a very limited collection of characters and speeches; unfortunately for auditionees, they have to perform those well-known speeches exceptionally well to succeed amongst the incredible competition. Experienced auditioners will have already seen a brilliant Juliet, Portia (either from *Julius Caesar* or *The Merchant of Venice*), Viola and Hermione, to mention but a few, against which we inevitably compare yours. If you use one of the well-known speeches at audition, unless you manage to hit that magic peak of performance, you are on an inevitable slope to failure.

Why do people stick to these popular speeches? I'm convinced that it's largely because they cannot face the idea of getting their heads round unfamiliar plays and characters written in obscure language. It's easier if you already have some idea of the character and play – from studying it at school, seeing a stage production or a film version. I estimate that nearly fifty per cent of *The Complete Works* are rarely performed. There is, sitting there unregarded, a great wealth of material from which the auditionee can draw. Why are they 'rarely performed'? Often, because they aren't as good as the famous plays, but they do contain material which is on a par with the greatest moments in Shakespeare. Sometimes, they are 'rarely performed' because the language is especially difficult (*Love's Labours Lost*, for instance), or because the historical knowledge required to follow the plot is too much for a modern audience (the *Henry VI* plays, for instance), or because the stories on which the plays are based are no longer part of our common culture (*Troilus and Cressida*, for instance). Shakespeare's audiences would not only have understood the jokes and topical references, but also would have had a working knowledge of their recent monarchs. Greek and Roman history, classical mythology, religious practices, and the Bible would all be much more familiar to them than they are to us now.

Even the well-known plays have lesser known, but not necessarily less interesting, characters in them. For instance, Olivia and Viola from *Twelfth Night* are very popular audition fare, but in this same delightful play is also the significant (but ignored for audition) Maria, a gentlewoman attending Olivia.

The other fundamental problem for the auditionee is length. Most people don't realise that fourteen or fifteen lines of verse is often perfectly sufficient (providing it also conforms to the other parameters mentioned in the 'Auditioning Shakespeare' chapter). Just because the famous speeches go on for twice or three times this length it doesn't mean that they mark an 'industry standard'. I suspect that Shakespeare wrote far fewer long speeches for his women because the boys who played them largely didn't have the skills to sustain such lengths of speech. I appreciate that it is especially difficult for women to find 'original' Shakespeare speeches, but as I hope this book proves, they are there – especially if you look at suitable dialogue and edit it to make a single speech (the Maria speeches mentioned above, for instance). Some people believe the idea of editing Shakespeare is tantamount to sacrilege. I think that this is ridiculous because there is no such thing as a definitive Shakespeare text (this is true for the vast majority of plays; most playwrights have alternative versions to that which arrives in print) and also in doing an audition you are performing a mini-play separated from the whole work and it therefore will lose some of the constraints that tied it in its original context. On the other hand editing dialogue is not necessarily simply cutting out the other person's lines. It requires time, thought and trying out to see whether or not it works.

Another thorny problem is punctuation. I largely worked from five different editions of each play and in my researches to date I have not yet found any sustained section of speech which is punctuated the same way in any two given editions. I have tried to rethink the punctuation to suit the modern actor, and I have a pious hope that Shakespeare might largely have approved of what I've done – after all he was working with actors, not academics. There are a number of instances where some words also vary between editions, and when there is an important alternative I have mentioned it in the notes.

Line numbering also varies, so I have chosen to number each speech from one. There are only a few instances where this is true of the speech in the play.

I have written notes on everything that might be obscure, but not following the dictates of any one academic editor. You will find I disagree with them all in a few instances. I also looked up every unfamiliar or obscure word in the *Oxford English Dictionary*, which was incredibly useful in illuminating the language. Overall I have tried to help you understand the details of each speech in order to perform it, rather than to write essays about it.

I have also included a short character description for each speech. These are meant to help kick you off in the task of reading the whole play. They are inevitably sketchy and only give the basics leading up to the moment of the speech. I cannot stress too much the fact that there is no substitute for reading and absorbing the whole play.

I have used the word 'actor' throughout this book, in spite of the fact that it's dedicated to women – after all, you don't talk about a 'doctor-ess' or a 'solicitor-ess', do you?

This is my second collection of fifty speeches which are rarely, if ever, used in audition. At the time of writing, I've also got another half-a-dozen up my sleeve and I know I'll be able to find more given time – you can too.

Finally, I would like to thank all those who helped me by work-shopping all these speeches before they were committed to print: Mellisa James, Jessica Radcliffe, Sophie Ridley, Lottie Roach and Aimie Worsnop; my mother, Alison Dunmore, for supplying me with tit-bits from her decades of watching Shakespeare in performance, and my wife, Maev Alexander, for her detailed and incisive comments on everything.

Female Characters and Speeches Too Often Used in Audition

Helena (*All's Well That Ends Well*)
Phoebe (*As You Like It*)
Rosalind (*As You Like It*)
Adriana (*The Comedy of Errors*)
Luciana (*The Comedy of Errors*)
Imogen (*Cymbeline*)
Gertrude (*Hamlet*)
Joan la Pucelle (*Henry VI, part 1*)
Queen Margaret (*Henry VI, parts 1, 2* and *3* and *Richard III*)
Lady Percy (*Henry IV, part 2*)
Queen Katherine (*Henry VIII*) – the court speeches (Act 2, Scene 4)
Portia (*Julius Caesar*)
Constance (*King John*)
Goneril (*King Lear*)
Lady Macbeth (*Macbeth*)
Isabella (*Measure for Measure*)
Portia (*The Merchant of Venice*)
Helena (*A Midsummer Night's Dream*)
Hermia (*A Midsummer Night's Dream*)
Puck (*A Midsummer Night's Dream*)
Titania (*A Midsummer Night's Dream*)
Beatrice (*Much Ado About Nothing*)
Emilia (*Othello*) – the 'Yes, a dozen...' speech (Act 4, Scene 3)
Marina (*Pericles*)
Lady Anne (*Richard III*) – the funeral scene speeches (Act 1, Scene 2)
Juliet (*Romeo and Juliet*)
The Nurse (*Romeo and Juliet*)
Katherine (*The Taming of the Shrew*)
Olivia (*Twelfth Night*)
Viola (*Twelfth Night*)
Julia (*The Two Gentlemen of Verona*)
The Jailer's Daughter (*The Two Noble Kinsmen*)
Hermione (*The Winter's Tale*)

I have cited specific scenes / speeches against a character, where there is material elsewhere for that character which is not too often used. This list is by no means exhaustive – other auditioners will have other characters and speeches they've seen too often.

Shakespeare – The Actors' Writer

Shakespeare, and others, wrote for a theatre that had minimal sets and an audience that did not sit quietly watching – they reacted like a modern football crowd. (Conditions that they are attempting to recreate at *The Globe Theatre* on London's South Bank.) He had no lighting beyond available daylight and the occasional flare or candle, no sophisticated special effects and no modern sound systems. There was some live music and the occasional drum, trumpet, cornet, and so on, but the principle emphasis was on the power of the excitingly spoken word. And that's what Shakespeare gave actors: a brilliant vehicle, his words, that can really help the auditioning actor – also without sets, lighting, and so on. He also had incredible insights into how people 'tick', in a way that wasn't really generally understood until about a hundred years ago – famously through Freud and in the acting world through Stanislavski. There is a story about a man after seeing his first Shakespeare production: 'Hey, this guy knew about Freud three-hundred years before Freud.'

Shakespeare the Man

We have a number of tantalising facts about the real person, but not enough to write a definitive biography. One thing we are sure of is that he managed to make a good living out of writing and staging plays – he had a commercial eye for what would attract audiences. He looked for popular subjects and managed to avoid controversy by writing plays set either remote in time and / or set in other countries. (Only *The Merry Wives of Windsor* is set overtly in the Elizabethan here-and-now, and that doesn't contain any kings, princes and so on – people who if offended could be highly dangerous.) He didn't write contemporary satires to attract audiences – unlike Ben Jonson, his friend and nearest rival as a playwright – and he seems to have avoided any trouble with the authorities, unlike Jonson who spent time in prison. I think that because he didn't have any political axe to grind, he concentrated on the people in his plays rather than contemporary politics. Issues relevant to an Elizabethan are largely only of interest to a historian of subsequent generations. I believe Shakespeare's apolitical approach and his concentration on the personalities involved

1

helped to ensure his immortality. I'm not saying that he didn't write about politics at all, his plays are full of examples; but he didn't take sides. For example, though there is a lot in *The Merchant of Venice* which is anti-Semitic (shockingly so to a modern audience), Shylock, the money-lender, has some wonderfully sympathetic moments including this (from Act 3, Scene 1): 'I am a Jew. Hath not a Jew eyes? Hath not a Jew hands, organs, dimensions, senses, affections, passions? Fed with the same food, hurt with the same weapons, subject to the same diseases, healed by the same means, warmed and cooled by the same winter and summer as a Christian is? If you prick us, do we not bleed? If you tickle us, do we not laugh? If you poison us, do we not die? And if you wrong us, shall we not revenge?'

As a playwright Shakespeare wasn't working in isolation, he was a member of several acting companies, principally the *Chamberlain's Men* (later known as the *King's Men*). I'd like to suggest that *The Complete Works* came not just from one man but through the energy and ideas generated by groups of people working closely together. A man called 'Shakespeare' may have written a lot of the words, but he must have used their experiences to inspire much of the detail. And, knowing actors, I'm sure they had plenty of their own suggestions – good and bad – that were incorporated into the scripts we now have. This is the cradle, the sustenance and encouragement that nurtured the 'genius' we label 'Shakespeare'. Over half a century later another genius, Sir Isaac Newton, the scientist, wrote, 'If I have seen further it is by standing on the shoulders of giants.' I suggest the same could be said of Shakespeare and his plays.

Elizabethan England

Not only was he almost certainly helped by his actors, but also by the comparatively stable political climate of the first Elizabethan age. As often happens in his history plays, the threat of invasion (and vice-versa) was common in the reigns of Queen Elizabeth I's predecessors. This required armies and ships, which were a huge drain on the national exchequer and when she ascended the throne England was not very well off. Her immediate predecessor (and elder sister), Mary, was a Catholic. Elizabeth, a Protestant, was a ripe target for Catholic France and Spain – England's principal rivals. There were also a number of people in England who thought that Protestantism had gone too far and would have welcomed an invasion. However, the two continental countries were at loggerheads and ignored England until the Spanish Armada in 1588, thirty years after Elizabeth had ascended the throne. In the interim the English ships had been used for lucrative trade and exploration, thus building a strong economy, strong enough to fund the soldiers and sailors for the defeat of the potential invaders by the time of the Armada; and strong enough to support the social welfare of the nation. 'We were just in a financial position to afford Shakespeare at the moment when he presented himself' (J. M. Keynes, Economist).

Elizabethan English

Elizabeth was the most extraordinary woman, highly intelligent and literate, and she used her power for the sake of the people, not just for her own ends, as most previous monarchs had done. She created a nation, with the help of some brilliant chief ministers, which had 'a zest and an energy and a love of life that had hardly been known before' (Anthony Burgess). This 'feel-good' factor, that modern politicians yearn for, created a new pride in the English language. Previously, Latin had held sway through the church, over the bulk of printed literature and throughout the limited education provision that existed then. People spoke to each other in various English dialects, but the use of the language in written form was extremely limited. Anything important was written in Latin, with its very strict rules of grammar and spelling – but there were virtually no official rules of spelling and grammar for English. Witness, the varying spellings that we have of Shakespeare's own name: 'Shaxpere', 'Shogspar', 'Choxper', and so on. These arise because each writer of the name (or any word) would write down the sound of what he'd heard as he would like to spell it. The written English of that time was 'not fixed and elegant and con-trolled by academics' (Anthony Burgess) – it was a language ripe for exploration and development, as the sailors were doing with material goods in the new world.

All this lack of regulation means that it is very common for Shakespeare's characters to commit what we would now consider to be grammatical howlers, for instance plural subjects combined with singular verbs and seemingly non-sensical changes in tense. However, he was writing (in elevated form) in the way people speak and these 'howlers' often reflect the characters' state of mind.

3

The Plots of Shakespeare's Plays

The commercial playwright had to write plays that he could be reasonably sure would attract an audience and took his plots from existing sources that would be generally known and appeal to a paying public. Early works included: *The Comedy of Errors*, a free adaptation of a well known Roman comedy of confused identity and *Titus Andronicus*, a sex and sadism horror that would put today's film censors into a complete spin. The three parts of *Henry VI* and *Richard III* are based on historical accounts of one of England's most troubled times which were finally resolved by acquisition of the throne by Henry VII, grandfather of the ever-popular Queen Elizabeth I – an event which happens at the end of *Richard III*. A modern equivalent might be dramatically to chart Winston Churchill's life from his 'wilderness years' (forced out of politics) to the triumph of the surrender of Nazi Germany.

Another aspect of this commercialism was the 'megabucks' that could be made by special one-off performances for rich patrons. For example, *Macbeth* was probably written for performance before King James I (Elizabeth I's successor). Banquo, one of Macbeth's victims in the play, was reputedly an ancestor of James; Shakespeare radically altered the available historical record to ensure that the King was not offended and included references to witchcraft, breast-feeding and tobacco – subjects very close to James' heart.

Some Significant Speeches in Shakespeare's Plays

It's not just the plots that Shakespeare adapted from known sources, he even adapted other people's words. For example in the court scene of *Henry VIII* (Act 2, Scene 4), Queen Katherine's wonderful speech beginning 'Sir, I desire you do me right and justice...' is an almost direct copy of what she actually said, according to the historical record. Enobarbus' famous speech 'The barge she sat in...' in *Antony and Cleopatra* (Act 2, Scene 2) is very close to a translation from Plutarch's *Life of Antonius*.

Shakespeare's Texts

Four hundred years on, it is difficult to be sure that every word in a Shakespeare play is exactly as he first wrote it. The problems with his play-texts begin with the fact that then there was no such thing as a law of copyright. That wasn't to arrive for another hundred years. Once a play was in print, anyone could simply copy and sell their own version with no royalties going to the original writer. Worse than this, once in print, other companies could put on their own productions in competition. So Shakespeare himself had very few of his own plays printed. About five years after Shakespeare's death, two of his actors John Heminge and Henry Condell put together what scripts they had into print: *The First Folio*, the first – nearly – *Complete Works*.

Amongst their sources were:

(a) Some of the original hand-written cue-scripts (just the individual actor's lines and his cue lines).

(b) Some previously published editions of individual plays, the 'Quarto' editions. ('Quarto' literally means the size of a piece of paper created by folding a whole sheet twice so as to form four leaves or eight pages. 'Folio' means folding that sheet once to make two leaves or four pages.)

(c) The memories of surviving actors.

None of these can be sworn to being entirely accurate because:

(a) Even the best handwriting of the time is sometimes hard to decipher. (We don't have any texts in Shakespeare's own hand.)

(b) Printing in his time wasn't entirely accurate. Think of having to place every letter, space and punctuation mark – each in the form of an individually-moulded piece of lead – into a frame that then went onto the presses. *The Complete Works* (with *The Two Noble Kinsmen*, which is not always included) total about 950,000 words, which is over five million characters; i.e. an average of roughly 25,000 words and 137,000 characters per play. Also some of the Quarto editions were printed from manuscripts written down during performances by people trying to 'pirate' the plays (often known as 'Bad Quartos').

(c) Sometimes actors have very accurate memories for lines they've said on stage; sometimes they improve on what the playwright actually wrote down; and sometimes, the lesser ones make a hash of the playwright's intentions.

Shakespeare probably didn't write every word anyway. There are at least four other writers who almost certainly contributed to what we now know as *The Complete Works*. It also seems to me likely given the circumstances in which Shakespeare wrote – for a specific company of actors – that they might well each have had their individual 'say' in the details of what their characters said and some of their ideas incorporated.

Further confusion is added by the fact that just one copy of a 'Quarto' or 'Folio' edition would be printed, proof-read and corrected, then a second copy would be printed, proof-read and corrected, and so on. Nobody knows whether these time-consuming processes were undertaken for every individual copy, but (to date) nobody has yet found two identical copies of *The First Folio* from the roughly 230 that survive.

There has been such a mass of intellectual detective work trying to establish a perfect version of the text that I believe it is easy to get the impression of a super-human being whose works must be approached with over-weening reverence. Shakespeare was a human being like the rest of us. He was possessed of a brilliant feel for the use of language and how people really feel deep down inside.

I do not say all this to try to bring Shakespeare down from his pedestal; I say it to humanise a man whom others have deified. I don't deny that a nation needs her heroes, but I think that England has elevated 'The Bard' overmuch. True he was part of an innovative (even revolutionary) group that has rarely been matched for its degree of positive development. But, in order to bring life back to his works, nearly four centuries after his death, we have to feel for him – as a jobbing craftsman needing to sell his wares to make a living. We need to make his creations have real life, rather than being some too often regurgitated ceremony that sounds stale.

Finally, I have to add that without the presiding genius and humanity of Elizabeth I we almost certainly wouldn't have known anything of him at all. Periods of great art arise when the prevailing governments are prepared to invest in their nation's culture.

The Lives and Times of Shakespeare's People

It is obvious to say that life was very different for people in Shakespeare's time. To recreate his characters it is important to have some insight into how 'different'.

Birth and Death

It was quite normal for a baby and / or the mother to die at or soon after birth. It is really only since the second world war that such deaths have become rare in Western society. Even if the child survived the crucial early period, many only managed it to their teens. A working class family would aim to breed as many children as possible as workers to help the family's meagre fortunes. Many women, even if they survived the multiple births, were dead of exhaustion by their thirties. The men had the hazard of the frequent wars. Medicine was very rudimentary – if not grotesquely inaccurate – and too expensive for all but the aristocracy, so disease and malnutrition meant that people, on average, lived about forty years. You were considered grown up by about the age of fourteen and old by your mid-thirties.

The aristocracy were better fed and had access to what medicine was available, but their chances in childbirth weren't much better and overall life-expectancy wasn't that much greater. (Though, the real Richard III's mother managed to live until she was eighty.)

Contraception was available (in fact the first evidence of its use dates back nearly four thousand years), but was generally only used for illicit sex. (A pig's bladder for the men and half a lemon for the women, for instance.)

Marriage

In Elizabethan England the age of consent was twelve and it was common for women to give birth in their early teens. Lady Capulet says to her fourteen year old daughter Juliet:

Well, think of marriage now. Younger than you
Here in Verona, ladies of esteem,
Are made already mothers. By my count
I was your mother much upon these years
That you are now a maid. (*Romeo and Juliet*, Act 1, Scene 3)

7

Prior to this period dynastic marriages often took place at even younger ages – for example, the real Richard II's wife, Isabel, was seven when she married him. This occurred when important families wanted to expand their power and possessions by alliance through marriage – equivalent to modern corporate mergers. The marriage partners often had no say in the course of events designed for them.

Democracy

Although the idea of running England through a democratic system started to evolve some three hundred years before Shakespeare, the monarch was still very much in charge – if he or she was strong and ruthless enough. Parliament consisted of the nobility, senior churchmen and representatives of the general population. However, it wasn't a democracy as we would now think of it; more a collection of power groupings who used military muscle to get their way. The nobility had the threat of their private armies; the church (prior to Henry VIII's break with the Roman Catholic church) could threaten to call on military aid from fellow catholic countries. There were also representatives from each town big enough and two knights from each shire (or county) – but these people couldn't call on armies to back up a point, so they had very little actual influence on major issues. Right up to the latter half of the nineteenth century only a small proportion of the male population of the 'civilised' world was allowed to vote; a certain level of wealth and / or literacy being the usual qualification. In Great Britain women had to wait until the twentieth century to be allowed to vote.

Law and Order

There was no national police force and the legal system was fairly arbitrary – generally, favouring the rich. It was comparatively easy to commit and cover up crimes, if you were clever about it. It was also fairly easy to be arrested for something you hadn't done if you were vulnerable and someone with the necessary finances wanted you imprisoned.

Travel and Communications

The only forms of land travel were either on foot or using a four footed animal, the horse being much the fastest. The latter were too expensive for the ordinary man and consequently the majority of ordinary people would never leave their home town or village.

Even those who became soldiers would travel by foot. All this meant that transmitting messages and moving armies took an inordinate amount of time.

Even someone with exceptionally fast horses could only travel at an average of about twenty miles an hour, so it would take at least a day to travel from London to York, for instance. If you did ride far, only stopping to change to fresh horses, you'd be utterly wrecked by the time you got there.

Taxation

In medieval times the monarch really only needed taxes to pay for wars, his general living expenses came from income from property he owned. By Shakespeare's time the tax system was more extensive in order also to pay for the ever expanding machinery of government. The ruling powers would, arbitrarily, invent a tax to cover an immediate financial problem. The concept of 'fairness' in taxation doesn't really occur until the late eighteenth century and 'income tax' was first introduced in 1799.

The Church

The church had enormous influence on people's lives, the power of the concept of 'God' was all prevailing – with no alternative view on the way the world worked. All but the most widely read would not challenge the idea that in order to have a good 'after life', you'd have to conform to the church's dictates in this life. Science was only just beginning to question some of the church's teachings – coincidentally, a prime-mover of this 'questioning', Galileo Galilei, was born in the same year as Shakespeare (1564), though it wasn't until the year of Shakespeare's death (1616) that he was taken to task by the church authorities for his revolutionary ideas.

It is also worth mentioning that the other most wonderful publication during the reign of King James I was the English language version of the Bible, which was still in common use until very recently.

Education

Education was just beginning to expand. It wasn't just the wealthy who could learn to read and write. Free schools were opening up, paid for by more enlightened boroughs and open to children of worthy local citizens, i.e. the elite of the middle-classes. The lessons consisted mostly of Latin studies, the language in which most of the limited printed matter of that time was issued; and a drilling in of their duties toward God, the sovereign and 'all others in their degree'. The poor had to wait until the late nineteenth century for the right to universal education.

Sanitation

Even in London there was no such thing as main drainage systems; sewage was simply dumped in the street – to be carried away by the rains, when they happened. Plague was a regular occurrence and when it struck, public places such as theatres were closed to prevent further infection. Country areas, like Shakespeare's Stratford, smelt sweeter and people's health was generally better than in the then cramped and stinking London.

Light and Heat

Burning what you could acquire was the only source of these basics; there were no national fuel grids of any kind.

Primitive but survivable, England was just moving from an aristocratically run society to one where even the lowliest individual was beginning to matter – only thirty-three years after Shakespeare died, the English executed their king and parliament ruled without an absolute monarch for eleven years.

Within the confines of this book I can only briefly evoke a few basic aspects of life in Shakespeare's time. A character's life is not just battles and loves, won and lost. It is also the ordinary, everyday aspects that the dramatist misses out because they are not dramatic and don't serve the life of the play. In order to bring those characters to life you should find out as much as you can about how their lives were lived outside the action of the play.

Auditioning Shakespeare

Shakespeare acting – at root – is not different from 'modern' acting. Where it is different is in that his language uses words, phrases and expressions we no longer use; and (more importantly) the circumstances are invariably far away from our direct experience. It is your job (whether aspiring or professional) to steep yourself in the culture that influenced his plays if you are to perform pieces from them.

Many actors argue that doing an audition speech is a desperately artificial way of having their worth assessed. I would tend to agree but, however much you may hate them, you will periodically have to do them. Of course it's an artificial situation, but isn't acting about making artifice seem real? There are ways of making them work – think of Bob Hoskins in *Who Framed Roger Rabbit* and Steve Martin in *Dead Men Don't Wear Plaid*, both acting with beings who weren't really there.

I have 'road-tested' all the speeches contained in this book; it is now your job to research and rehearse those of your choice. You also need to prepare yourself for the varying circumstances you could be asked to perform them in. Think of an audition speech as a 'mini-play'; you are going to present a 'mini-production' of it.

PREPARATIONS
There are a number of things to consider before you start rehearsing your speeches:

Iambic Pentameters
Apart from the unfamiliar words, phrases and expressions, this verse form (popular in Shakespeare's time) is off-putting – on the page – to many people. I think it's a good idea to think of it not as poetry, but as verbal music: that is words and phraseology that people use when they have a real need to express themselves or 'touch the souls of others'. A good playwright not only writes good stories and creates credible characters, but also writes in language that will 'grab' an audience – language that has a music of its own. Shakespeare was a master of verbal music, along with Samuel Beckett, Harold Pinter, Sam Shepard, Edward Albee, David Mamet, Arthur Miller, Alan Ayckbourn, and too many more to mention. It is not so much plots that make great playwrights, it is their use of language.

Rhymes

Some of the verse rhymes, which can sound terribly forced and unnatural if you emphasise the rhyming words too much. You can't avoid the rhyme, but it's important to make it sound natural and not forced (as poetry is often read).

-èd

All the accent on the 'e' means is that you pronounce the 'ed' where you normally wouldn't. For example: we'd normally pronounce 'imagined' not sounding the 'e'; but if it's written 'imaginèd', you pronounce it 'imagin-ed'. Some editions miss out the 'e' if it is not to be pronounced and insert an apostrophe instead and leave it there, unaccented, if it should be sounded.

i', th', and so on

Some people balk at these foreshortened words. All this means is that you pronounce them literally as written. Listen to yourself and others in normal conversation and note how many letters we miss out.

Making Sense

As you start out on a speech look at the sense, ignore the verse. Look for the full stops, even if they arrive halfway through a line. Then, look at each clause within that sentence; then put that whole sentence together to make the sense of the whole of it. Then, start to put the sense of the whole speech together – still ignoring the verse.

Finally, look at what words begin and end a line of verse, they may have a significance that you haven't previously recognised. After you've been through all the processes of finding and becoming the character, the positioning of these words may add to your understanding of her.

'The multitudinous seas incarnadine' (*Macbeth*, Act 2, Scene 2)

In his musical on the life of William Blake, *Tyger*, Adrian Mitchell had Shakespeare appear as a cowboy, or 'pen-slinger': 'I can drop 'em with one line'. It's that turn of phrase (that has now degraded into the 'sound-bite') that makes Shakespeare's language so exciting. It is your job also to make it 'real' for the character – don't sing it, believe it.

Preconceptions

With the famous characters, forget any preconceived notions you may have, e.g. Hamlet is 'mad', Juliet is 'wet', and so on. Part of Shakespeare's insight is that he created (mostly) very real people who may primarily exhibit one aspect of human behaviour through the circumstances of the play; but, as in life, there's far more to them than that. Think how often you meet someone new and form an instant impression, then you get the chance to get to know them and find that there's 'far more than meets the eye'. The aim of this book is to steer people away from these too well-known characters, but the same kind of preconception can take over and dominate the performance. For instance, Dionyza (from *Pericles*) seems like a classic 'baddie', but in her eyes she has good reasons for wanting rid of Marina – fundamentally she wants the world better for her own daughter; a good maternal instinct. It's her means that seem extreme to us, but in Shakespeare's time she would have had a very good chance of getting away with Marina's murder – life was cheap.

Selecting Speeches

Read through the speeches in this book and see which ones create sparks for you, without necessarily fully understanding the content. (Largely, ignore the notes and character description at first, these come later.) If the 'music' of the words feels good then you are over halfway towards finding a speech suitable for you. It can also be a good idea to read them – carefully – out loud, without any sense of 'acting' them. Then read the 'Character Descriptions' to see if the characters are appropriate to you (age, type, and so on) and assess whether it's worth going further.

Don't be tempted simply to go for ones with the most spectacular emotions – auditioners want to see real feelings not flashy melodrama.

Length

An audition speech doesn't need to be more than about two minutes long and can be shorter, which can feel too short whilst you are doing it. Interestingly, Shakespeare speeches often work better when they're even shorter; I think that it may be something to do with the fact that he packs so much into his characters – a few of his words can speak such volumes. Many people think that they're not doing enough with thirteen to fifteen lines of verse – which will probably last only about sixty to ninety seconds. Providing the speech has a complete journey to it, it doesn't matter if it's this short. On the other hand, you can lose your audience if you go on for forty lines. You may argue that there is no way you can show enough of your skills as an actor in such a short time. True, you can't show everything, but you can give a very good indication of your potential – like a good television commercial.

How Many?

For too many people the 'Shakespeare' is the speech they least want to do, and they strain even to get the minimum (of one) together. I think this is very silly. The best results I've seen have come from people who've worked on four or five – and even more. Especially if you are new to acting in his language (as opposed to just reading it), working on several speeches at once can give you a much broader insight into his world. And if you begin to fall out of love with one or two of them, you've got the others to fall back on. If you only start with one, you've got to start all over again if you become dissatisfied with it.

Verse or Prose

Some auditioners insist that you present verse speeches, so it is important to have at least one in your repertoire.

Read the Whole Play

Next, read the whole play (slowly and carefully), read a few commentaries and if possible talk about the play and its people with someone who knows it. It can be helpful to read a summary first and then read the play, but bear in mind that these merely sum up the major plot and what happens to the people, without giving much psychological insight.

When a play is completely new to me, I find it helpful to copy out the cast list and write notes about each character as they appear.

Obviously this takes time, but it's extremely helpful to the process of getting under the skins of the characters.

On the other hand, don't spend hours flicking backwards and forwards to the footnotes to try to understand every line. A general sense of the people and events is all that's needed at this stage (and how your character fits in). It's important to get some idea of the flow of the whole thing – too much stopping and starting can make you lose any idea of the whole.

It is not sufficient just to read the scene a chosen speech is from – you won't gain proper insight into where your character is coming from.

The Immediate Context

When you've got hold of who your 'person' is, build up the stimuli that affect her: the other people (present and / or influential), the circumstances (place, time, and so on) – as well as the immediate provocation for the speech.

The Details

One of the fundamental keys to good acting is the degree of detail with which you imagine the above. For example, if your character is in a castle, it's not any old castle, it's somebody's home – maybe your character's own. Look at pictures and, if possible, visit castles that are preserved as they were lived in (ruins will only give a partial impression). Try to absorb the details of what it might have been like to live in one. (Touch bare stone walls, that'll give you a very strong feel for medieval living.) In short, find out (and imagine, if you can't find out) as much as you can about the 'ordinary' bits of the life your character might have led that are not mentioned in the play.

The Clothes

A supremely important 'detail' is the clothes your character(s) would wear. I'm not suggesting that you dress in period clothes, but to imagine the feel of wearing them. One of the principal omissions I see, is the sense of wearing a skirt that goes right down to the ground. It is only in the last hundred years that skirt-lengths have started to rise above that level. Different clothes, including shoes, make you move in different ways.

The Notes

Begin to understand the details of the words and phrases of the speech through using my notes and those from a good edition of the complete play. (See my Bibliography at the end of this book for suggestions on this). Write out your own translation into modern English if you find that useful, but don't become wedded to that translation, you'll find it hard to go back to the original. It's probably best to write it out and then throw it away, so you get a better idea of the sense without becoming fixed on specific modern words and phrases.

The notes attached to some established editions can confuse with cross-references irrelevant to acting; they may be written 'about' the character, rather than for the person acting her. On the other hand, the notes in some exam text 'note' books can tend to over-simplify.

Research

When there are real people involved it can be useful to research what we now know about them. However, Shakespeare had a rather 'tabloid' attitude to the truth. The 'history plays' are based on real historical events (*Henry VIII* ends only thirty-one years before Shakespeare's birth), but, like many other playwrights since he doesn't always follow historical facts as we now understand them. Sometimes this is because the then limited historical research was inaccurate; sometimes it is because reality doesn't necessarily make good drama (common to all drama); sometimes (especially in *Henry VIII*) he couldn't risk the wrath of current sensibilities; and possibly, sometimes because he was writing too fast to research properly or he was simply lazy. Do research, but don't let historical inaccuracies confuse you: take what you can from history but the information gleaned from the play must finally be the deciding factor.

Learning the Lines

Don't sit down and learn the lines parrot fashion. In all this research into the background detail, keep going back to the play, your character and her speech, to check that what you've found out (and used your imagination to create) still fits with what's in the text. You will find those lines simply start 'going in' the more you understand them and the circumstances of them being spoken.

If you find that parts will not 'go in' by this process of study and absorption, then it is almost certain that you haven't fully under-stood what they mean.

Don't Generalise!

Because it's a speech too may people tend to generalise, and it all comes out sounding the same. In life very few people anticipate speaking at such length except in specific circumstances. You should think of it as a series of connected thoughts and ideas – the circumstances stimulate the first thought to come out as words, then another arrives and needs to be spoken, and another, and so on. Usually, at the beginning, you should convey the impression you don't know what you are going to say at the end.

Soliloquies

Shakespeare is famous for these and some people think that they should always be addressed to the audience. With obvious excep-tions (the 'Chorus' and some of the clowns, for instance), I believe they are the characters talking to themselves – 'for' the audience. When we talk to ourselves in life we keep it private and mutter. In acting we have to communicate to an audience – this is one of the fundamental differences between the 'being' process above and acting. You've got to go through the first stage of 'being' before you can go on to 'act' your speech. Don't try to prepare the other way round.

It's useful to think of soliloquies as the character thinking aloud in order to try to organise her jumbled thoughts.

Difficult to Say Words and Phrases

If you find yourself consistently tripping over a word or phrase, try saying it in isolation – with a lot of over-articulation. Do this slowly and carefully lots of times and you'll find it'll become second nature to you.

Obscure Words and Phrases

I am still amazed by the fact that if the actor understands these – in her soul – the general sense will communicate to whatever audience is watching, and they don't need extra demonstration. This 'understanding' is not simply a mental process, it is a feeling for what the word or phrase means so that it becomes a totally natural thing to say in the circumstances.

First Steps

When you think that you know and understand what your character (or 'person') is talking about and understand their circumstances, start saying the lines out loud – aiming to talk to whoever is or are the recipients of the words. Don't think of it as acting; you are slowly beginning to become the 'person' who is saying those words – through the speaking of them combined with all your thinking and research. Take a line or two at a time, and go back over each small section several times until you begin to feel you are emotionally connecting. You should begin to see the circumstances really happening in your imagination. One (pre-drama school) student I taught was really getting inside a Richard II speech; suddenly he stopped and said, 'I can see those f****** horses!' I shouted, 'Keep going!' and when he finished we talked about his experience. The steady research and thought he had put in (over about two months) had paid off. After that he 'saw' those horses regularly when doing this speech, but it wasn't as shocking as the first time – just a normal part of 'being' Richard II. (Incidentally, he had no any idea of where this king fitted into English history when he started.)

When you are 'connecting' with your first line or two go on to the next, but use the first as a run up, and steadily on through the speech. (Please note that I still haven't suggested 'learning' the lines yet.)

I'm convinced that creating a character is very similar to the growing process from cradle to maturity.

Rehearsing Your Speeches

After you've done all this preparation you can start rehearsing your speeches, actually becoming the person saying those words in those particular circumstances. If you've prepared thoroughly, you'll be wonderfully surprised at how real, alive and exciting you can now make someone who was created four centuries ago.

Shakespeare's Advice

Hamlet says the following to a group of strolling players:

> Speak the speech, I pray you, as I pronounced it to you – trippingly on the tongue; but if you mouth it, as many of your players do, I had as lief the town-crier had spoke my lines. Nor do not saw the air too much with your hand, thus, but use all gently; for in the very torrent, tempest, and as I may say the whirlwind of your passion, you must acquire and beget a temperance that may give it smoothness. O, it offends me to the soul to hear a robustious, periwig-pated fellow tear a passion to tatters, to very rags, to split the ears of the groundlings, who for the most part are capable of nothing but inexplicable dumb shows and noise...
>
> ... Be not too tame, neither; but let your own discretion be your tutor. Suit the action to the word, the word to the action, with this special observance: that you o'erstep not the modesty of nature. For anything so overdone is from the purpose of playing, whose end, both at the first and now, was and is to hold as 'twere the mirror up to nature... Now this overdone, or come tardy off, though it make the unskilful laugh, cannot but make the judicious grieve... *(Hamlet*, Act 3, Scene 2)

This is some of the most succinct acting advice ever given – three hundred years before Stanislavski (and others) were completely rethinking how we achieve good acting.

The Speeches

All's Well That Ends Well

The Countess of Rossillion

The Countess of Rossillion is the mother of Bertram and Helena is her ward. Helena is in love with Betram and wants to marry him. At first he refuses her, but when the King orders that they should be married he gives way. However, Betram runs away to the wars before the marriage can be consummated and Helena decides that she must leave France so that her husband may live unhindered by an unwanted wife (Act 3, Scene 2). In this scene the Countess' steward, Reynaldo, has just read to her a letter from Helena telling her foster-mother of her departure and this is her response.

The Countess could be as young as mid-thirties, but is generally played older.

3	*her prayers* (She is referring to Helena.)
4	*greatest justice* the supreme Judge
	Reynaldo (He is Rynaldo or Rinaldo in some editions.)
5	*unworthy husband of his wife* husband unworthy of his wife
6	*weigh heavy of her worth* count as much as she is worthy (virtuous and self-sacrificing)
7	*weigh too light* values so lightly
8	*sharply* so as to make it absolutely clear (to Bertram)
9	*most convenient* fittest
10	*When haply* Perhaps when
14-15	*I have no skill in sense / To* I cannot on the basis of my feelings
17	*bids me speak* insists that I speak

20

Act 3, Scene 4
Countess –

1   What angel shall
        Bless this unworthy husband? He cannot thrive,
        Unless her prayers, whom heaven delights to hear
        And loves to grant, reprieve him from the wrath
        Of greatest justice. Write, write, Reynaldo,
5   To this unworthy husband of his wife.
        Let every word weigh heavy of her worth
        That he does weigh too light. My greatest grief,
        Though little he do feel it, set down sharply.
        Dispatch the most convenient messenger.
10   When haply he shall hear that she is gone,
        He will return; and hope I may that she,
        Hearing so much, will speed her foot again,
        Led hither by pure love. Which of them both
        Is dearest to me I have no skill in sense
15   To make distinction. Provide this messenger.
        My heart is heavy and mine age is weak;
17   Grief would have tears, and sorrow bids me speak.

                                    Exeunt

All's Well That Ends Well

Mariana

Mariana is a neighbour of Diana and her mother, the Widow Capilet, a Florentine innkeeper. The three women have come to see the arrival of the victorious French army led by Betram, Count of Rossillion. Diana and her mother briefly extol Betram's heroism, then they suddenly realise that the army has 'gone a contrary way'. Before they can think about trying to catch up with the French, Mariana stops them with this caution. This is her only scene and we learn no more about her, but she is obviously a woman of some experience of the world. She could be any age between twenties and forties.

I have constructed this speech from two of Mariana's, adapted a line of the Widow's and taken the final sentence from later in the scene.

1	*return again* return home
2 & 7	*Earl* (i.e. Bertram. 'Earl' is the English form of the continental title, 'Count'.)
3	*her name* her reputation (i.e. as a virgin.)
	honesty chastity
6	*Parolles* (He is pronounced *Pa-rol-ays* and has only one 'l' in some editions.)
6–7	*A filthy officer he is in those suggestions for the young Earl.* He is a disgusting go-between who leads girls astray for the young Earl.
8	*tokens* presents
	engines of lust devices designed to contrive seduction (*these* is 'their' in some editions)
9	*not the things they go under.* not what they appear to be.
11	*wrack* ruin (This is 'wreck' in some editions.)
11–12	*dissuade succession* prevent others from following the same course
12	*but that* unless
	limed with the twigs caught by the trap (Twigs were smeared with sticky bird-lime to catch young birds.)
14	*grace* virtue
14–16	*though there were no further danger known but the modesty which is so lost.* even if there were not also the risk of pregnancy.
16	*else* otherwise

Act 3, Scene 5
Mariana –

1   Come, let's return again, and suffice ourselves with the report
       of it. – Well, Diana, take heed of this French Earl. The honour
       of a maid is her name, and no legacy is so rich as honesty.
       Well, your mother has told me how you have been solicited
5   by a gentleman, his companion. I know that knave, hang
       him! One Parolles. A filthy officer he is in those suggestions
       for the young Earl. Beware of them, Diana: their promises,
       enticements, oaths, tokens, and all these engines of lust, are
       not the things they go under. Many a maid hath been seduced
10   by them; and the misery is, example, that so terrible shows in
       the wrack of maidenhood, cannot for all that dissuade
       succession, but that they are limed with the twigs that
       threatens them. I hope I need not to advise you further, but I
       hope your own grace will keep you where you are, though
15   there were no further danger known but the modesty which
16   is so lost. The gods forbid else!

Antony and Cleopatra

Charmian

Charmian is one of Cleopatra's attendants, along with Iras, Alexas and others. Of all of them Charmian is the closest to their mistress. She is lively, forthright and absolutely loyal to her mistress. When Cleopatra dies, Charmian straightens her mistress' crown before she kills herself in the same way.

At this point in the play Cleopatra's affair with Antony is at its height and there is a light-hearted atmosphere in her palace. Alexas has just told Charmian that a Soothsayer has arrived and has predictions of a husband for her. She could be any age between late teens and mid-thirties.

This speech is constructed from a number of shorter ones. I have also made a few slight word changes.

In some editions characters named Lamprius, Rannius, Lucillius and Mardian enter with those named in the stage directions but they say nothing during the scene – the first three say nothing throughout the play. There are variations in when the Soothsayer and Enobarbus (Antony's chief lieutenant) enter. I have presumed that the Soothsayer is already present when Charmian and the others enter the room.

1	*any thing* (This is 'anything' in some editions, I think it's more of a put-down with the two words separated.)
2	*absolute* perfect
3	*husband* (i.e. for Charmian.)
4	*charge his horns with garlands!* be a contented cuckold! ('Charge' is 'change' in some editions which changes the sense of the line.)
6	*Good now* Come on (good sir)
9	*Herod of Jewry* (Herod ordered the Slaughter of the Innocents in his attempt to kill the infant Christ – the last person in the world to do homage to an infant.)
	Find me to marry me Find (a sign in my palm) that I will marry
10	*Octavius Caesar* (One of the rulers of Rome and Antony's chief rival.)
	companion me with my mistress (Cleopatra had been mistress to Julius Caesar.)
11	*wenches* girls
11–12	*oily palm* (A moist or oily palm was believed to be a sign of a licentious nature.)
12	*fruitful prognostication* sign that I will have children
12–13	*I cannot scratch mine ear.* I am not a true woman. (To have itching ears meant to enjoy gossip, which was considered to be a specifically female trait.)
13	*her* (i.e. Iras)
	workaday (This is 'workday' in some editions.)
15	*cannot go* is frigid
15, 18 & 19	*Isis* (The Egyptian goddess of the moon and of fertility.)

Act 1, Scene 2
Charmian –

Alexandria. Cleopatra's palace.
Enter Charmian, Iras, Alexas and Enobarbus

1   Lord Alexas, sweet Alexas, most any thing Alexas, almost
     most absolute Alexas, where's the soothsayer that you
     praised so to th' Queen? O that I knew this husband, which
     you say must charge his horns with garlands! Is this the man?
5   Is't you, sir, that know things? [*Gives her hand to the
     Soothsayer*] Good sir, give me good fortune. Good now, some
     excellent fortune! Let me be married to three kings in a
     forenoon and widow them all. Let me have a child at fifty, to
     whom Herod of Jewry may do homage. Find me to marry me
10   with Octavius Caesar, and companion me with my mistress.
     Prithee, how many boys and wenches must I have? If an oily
     palm be not a fruitful prognostication, I cannot scratch mine
     ear. Prithee, tell her but a workaday fortune. And, Alexas –
     come, his fortune, his fortune! O, let him marry a woman that
15   cannot go, sweet Isis, I beseech thee! And let her die too, and
     give him a worse, and let worse follow worse till the worst of
     all follow him laughing to his grave, fiftyfold a cuckold.
     Good Isis, hear me this prayer, though thou deny me a matter
19   of more weight; good Isis, I beseech thee.

Antony and Cleopatra

Octavia

Octavia (d. 11 B.C.) was the sister of Octavius Caesar and was married to Antony as part of a treaty between Octavius and Antony. (The two men were part of the triumvirate that ruled the Roman Empire after the defeat of the assassins of Julius Caesar, Octavius' adoptive father.) With the onset of Antony's affair with Cleopatra (Queen of Egypt, which was part of the Roman Empire) the two men started to fall out and this marriage marked a temporary reconciliation. However, Antony has just heard that Octavius has been angling for more power for himself and speaking 'scantly' of Antony. He tells Octavia and this is her response. She is probably in her twenties.

In the play this is two speeches; I have also changed two words.

Part of this speech is adapted from one that Plutarch, a Roman historian, reports she made to Octavius.

---

3   *Stomach* Resent
4   *chance* occurs
5   *parts* (i.e. between Antony and Octavius Caesar.)
6   *presently* immediately
8   *Undo* And then undo

Act 3, Scene 4
Octavia –

1   O, my good lord,
        Believe not all; or, if you must believe,
        Stomach not all. A more unhappy lady,
        If this division chance, ne'er stood between,
5   Praying for both parts.
        The good gods will mock me presently,
        When I shall pray, 'O, bless my lord and husband!',
        Undo that prayer by crying out as loud,
        'O, bless my brother!' Husband win, win brother,
10   Prays and destroys the prayer; no midway
        'Twixt these extremes at all. O, good my lord
        The Jove of power make me most weak, most weak,
        Your reconciler! Wars 'twixt you twain would be
        As if the world should cleave, and that slain men
15   Should solder up the rift.

Antony and Cleopatra

Cleopatra

Cleopatra, Queen of Egypt (68–30 B.C.) met Antony when she was twenty-nine. She had previously been the mistress of Julius Caesar and of Gnaeus Pompey, the younger son of Pompey the Great (Caesar's arch rival).

Antony has been at war with his former ally Octavius Caesar (the adopted son of Julius Caesar) but when the Egyptian fleet deserts Antony realises that he cannot win. He rages at Cleopatra ('Triple-turned whore!'); she retreats to her monument. From there she sends word that she has committed suicide – a typical emotional trick for her to play. He tries to commit suicide but only succeeds in seriously wounding himself. He then learns that Cleopatra is still alive and orders that he be taken to her where he finally dies in her arms. Victorious Octavius sends Proculeius (whom Antony had previously said she could trust) to reassure her, but other Roman soldiers suddenly arrive and she tries to stab herself but is prevented. Proculeius tries to calm her down; she responds with this speech. Historically, she was thirty-eight at this point.

2	*If idle talk will once be necessary* Even if it is necessary for me to make trivial conversation (in order to stay awake)
3	*This mortal house* (i.e. her body)
5	*wait* serve
	pinioned trapped (Literally, like a bird with clipped wings.)
6	*once* ever
7	*Octavia* (Antony's wife.)
8	*varletry* common rabble
9	*censuring* judgmental
12	*Blow me into abhorring* Deposit their eggs on me and make me abhorrent
13	*pyramides* pyramids (This is the plural of the Latin 'pyramis' and is pronounced 'pyramidaze'.)

Act 5, Scene 2
Cleopatra –

1   Sir, I will eat no meat. I'll not drink, sir.
      If idle talk will once be necessary,
      I'll not sleep neither. This mortal house I'll ruin,
      Do Caesar what he can. Know, sir, that I
5   Will not wait pinioned at your master's court,
      Nor once be chastised with the sober eye
      Of dull Octavia. Shall they hoist me up
      And show me to the shouting varletry
      Of censuring Rome? Rather a ditch in Egypt
10   Be gentle grave unto me; rather on Nilus' mud
      Lay me stark nak'd, and let the waterflies
      Blow me into abhorring; rather make
      My country's high pyramides my gibbet,
14   And hang me up in chains.

Antony and Cleopatra

Cleopatra

Cleopatra, Queen of Egypt (68–30 B.C.) met Antony when she was twenty-nine. She had previously been the mistress of Julius Caesar and of Gnaeus Pompey, the younger son of Pompey the Great (Caesar's arch rival).

Antony has been at war with his former ally Octavius Caesar (the adopted son of Julius Caesar) but when the Egyptian fleet deserts Antony realises that he cannot win. He rages at Cleopatra ('Triple-turned whore!'); she retreats to her monument. From there she sends word that she has committed suicide – a typical emotional trick for her to play. He tries to commit suicide but only succeeds in seriously wounding himself. He then learns that Cleopatra is still alive and orders that he be taken to her where he finally dies in her arms. Victorious Octavius first sends Proculeius (whom Antony had previously said she could trust) to reassure her, but other Roman soldiers suddenly arrive and she tries to stab herself but is prevented. Proculeius tries to calm her down then Dolabella (another aide to Octavius) arrives to take over her guard. He tries again to calm her, but she suddenly starts into this rhapsody on her dead lover. Historically, she was thirty-eight at this point.

I have cut Dolabella's attempted interruptions to construct this speech.

4	*stuck* were set
6	*The little O, the earth*. (This is 'The little O o' th' earth' in some editions.)
7–8	*his reared arm / Crested the world* (This is an image from heraldry: a coat of arms could have a raised arm, sometimes holding a sword, as a crest.)
8–9	*was propertied / As* had the qualities of
9	*tunèd spheres* (There was a belief that as the seven planets rotated round the earth they each produced a musical note, and that together they produced a perfectly harmonious sound which was inaudible to human beings.)
	and that to friends when speaking to friends
10	*quail* terrify
	orb world
12	*an Antony it was* (This is 'an autumn 'twas' (or 'it was') in some editions.)
13–15	*His delights ... lived in.* Just as dolphins show their backs above the water ('element'), so Antony rose superior to the pleasures which were his element.
15	*livery* retinue (A livery was a suit of clothes given by a master to his servants as a token by which they could be identified.)
16	*crown and crownets* kings and princes
17	*plates* silver coins

Act 5, Scene 2
Cleopatra –

1   I dreamt there was an emperor Antony.
   O, such another sleep, that I might see
   But such another man!
   His face was as the heavens, and therein stuck
5   A sun and moon, which kept their course and lighted
   The little O, the earth.
   His legs bestrid the ocean; his reared arm
   Crested the world. His voice was propertied
   As all the tunèd spheres, and that to friends;
10   But when he meant to quail and shake the orb,
   He was as rattling thunder. For his bounty,
   There was no winter in 't; an Antony it was
   That grew the more by reaping. His delights
   Were dolphin-like; they showed his back above
15   The element they lived in. In his livery
   Walked crowns and crownets; realms and islands were
   As plates dropped from his pocket.
   Think you there was, or might be, such a man
19   As this I dreamt of?

Coriolanus

Volumnia

Volumnia is an aristocratic Roman matron and the mother of Caius Martius (a Roman general), who was given the name 'Coriolanus' at the beginning of the play, after his victory over the Volscians. She is predominant over her son ('There's no man in the world / More bound to 's mother') and manages to persuade (even bully) him to do things against his own will as the play progresses. Her upbringing has made him the successful (and arrogant) warrior that he is.

After five victories over the Volscians Coriolanus is nominated to become a Consul (the highest office in republican Rome), however he is grudging about going through the required processes of induction to the consulate – principally, the tradition of showing his scars to the common people. In this scene Volumnia is trying to persuade her son to swallow his pride and apologise for his arrogant behaviour. He has just said to her, 'Why force you this?'; this is her response. Volumnia is probably in her mid-forties, but is generally played older.

1	*it lies you on to* it is your responsibility to
1–9	(The lineation is different in some editions.)
2	*not by your own instruction* not as you'd really like to
4–5	*but roted in / Your tongue* simply memorised and recited (without feeling)
5–6	*bastards and syllables / Of no allowance to your bosom's truth.* (i.e. insincere words that you don't actually believe.)
8	*take in* capture
9	*put you to your fortune* force you to take your chances (in battle)
11	*dissemble with my nature where* be untrue to myself if
12	*at stake* at risk
13	*in honour* in accord with the requirements of honour
	I am in this I stand in this for
15	*will* would
	general common
16	*spend a fawn upon 'em* give them what they want
17	*inheritance* acquisition
18	*that want* (i.e. that failure to fawn)

Act 3, Scene 2
Volumnia –

1   Because that now it lies you on to speak
      To th' people, not by your own instruction,
      Nor by th' matter which your heart prompts you,
      But with such words that are but roted in
5   Your tongue, though but bastards and syllables
      Of no allowance to your bosom's truth.
      Now, this no more dishonours you at all
      Than to take in a town with gentle words,
      Which else would put you to your fortune and
10   The hazard of much blood.
      I would dissemble with my nature where
      My fortunes and my friends at stake required
      I should do so in honour. I am in this
      Your wife, your son, these senators, the nobles;
15   And you will rather show our general louts
      How you can frown, than spend a fawn upon 'em
      For the inheritance of their loves and safeguard
18   Of what that want might ruin.

Coriolanus

Volumnia

Volumnia is an aristocratic Roman matron and the mother of Caius Martius (a Roman general), who was given the name 'Coriolanus' at the beginning of the play, after his victory over the Volscians. She is predominant over her son ('There's no man in the world / More bound to 's mother') and manages to persuade (even bully) him to do things against his own will as the play progresses. Her upbringing has made him the successful (and arrogant) warrior that he is.

After five victories over the Volscians Coriolanus is nominated to become a Consul (the highest office in republican Rome), however he is grudging about going through the required processes of induction to the consulate – principally he rejects the requirement that the common people (the 'rabble') have a voice in his election. His pride and arrogance eventually lead to his banishment from Rome. He has not long departed from the city and Volumnia (accompanied by Coriolanus' wife, Virgilia, and Menenius, his friend and adviser) has just encountered Brutus and Sicinius two of her son's principal opponents. This is part of her rant against the two men. Volumnia is probably in her mid-forties, but is generally played older.

I have edited several speeches together to construct this speech.

1	*incensed the rabble* (Against Coriolanus.)
2	*Cats* (This is a general expression of contempt.)
14	*unclog* unburden
16	*Leave* Cease
	faint puling feeble whimpering
17	*Juno-like* (i.e. magnificently; Juno was the chief goddess of the Romans and wife of Jupiter.)

Act 4, Scene 2
Volumnia –

1   Bastards and all! 'Twas you incensed the rabble –
     Cats that can judge as fitly of his worth
     As I can of those mysteries which heaven
     Will not have earth to know.
5   Now pray, sir, get you gone.
     You have done a brave deed. Ere you go, hear this:
     As far as doth the Capitol exceed
     The meanest house in Rome, so far my son –
     This lady's husband here, this, do you see? –
10   Whom you have banished does exceed you all.
                                    Exeunt Brutus and Sicinius

     Take my prayers with you.
     I would the gods had nothing else to do
     But to confirm my curses. Could I meet 'em
     But once a day, it would unclog my heart
15   Of what lies heavy to it. [*To Virgilia*] Come, let's go.
     Leave this faint puling and lament as I do,
17   In anger, Juno-like. Come, come, come.
                                    Exeunt Volumnia and Virgilia

Cymbeline

The Queen of Britain

The Queen of Britain is the wife of King Cymbeline and stepmother of his daughter Imogen, and mother (by a former marriage) of the oafish Cloten. She wants to see him married to Imogen so as to secure the throne for him. However, Imogen has secretly married Posthumus who is then banished. His faithful servant, Pisanio, stays behind to serve Imogen. The Queen has just received, what she believes, is a potent poison (in a 'box') from a doctor (Cornelius) when Pisanio arrives. She dismisses the doctor and begins by trying to recruit Pisanio to convince Imogen to forget her husband and marry Cloten. Pisanio does not respond and she 'drops' the box and continues with this.

Although King Cymbeline really existed (generally called Cunobelius) around two thousand years ago, we know nothing about his real queen. She could be any age from early thirties to early fifties.

This is part of a very long speech which is far too long to use in its entirety for audition.

4	*cordial* stimulating
5	*earnest* reward (in expectation of further)
	further (This is 'farther' in some editions.)
8	*Think what a chance thou changest on* Think of the risk ('chance') if you do change ('changest') your loyalties
9	*to boot* even better
12	*thou'lt* you will (thou wilt)
13	*desert* course of action
16	*shaked* turned (in his loyalties)
17	*remembrancer* reminder (to her to remain true to her husband)
18	*hand-fast* contract of marriage
20	*liegers* ambassadors
21	*bend her humour* change her mood (and disinclination towards Cloten)

Act 1, Scene 6 (Scene 5 in some editions)
Queen –

She drops her box. Pisanio takes it up

1   Thou tak'st up
     Thou know'st not what; but take it for thy labour.
     It is a thing I made, which hath the King
     Five times redeemed from death. I do not know
     What is more cordial. Nay, I prithee take it.
5   It is an earnest of a further good
     That I mean to thee. Tell thy mistress how
     The case stands with her; do 't as from thyself.
     Think what a chance thou changest on, but think
     Thou hast thy mistress still; to boot, my son,
10   Who shall take notice of thee. I'll move the King
     To any shape of thy preferment, such
     As thou'lt desire; and then myself, I chiefly,
     That set thee on to this desert, am bound
     To load thy merit richly. Call my women.
15   Think on my words. [*Exit Pisanio*] A sly and constant knave,
     Not to be shaked; the agent for his master,
     And the remembrancer of her to hold
     The hand-fast to her lord. I have given him that
     Which, if he take, shall quite unpeople her
20   Of liegers for her sweet; and which she after,
     Except she bend her humour, shall be assured
22   To taste of too. Fare thee well, Pisanio.

Cymbeline

The Queen of Britain

The Queen of Britain is the wife of King Cymbeline and mother (by a former marriage) of the oafish Cloten. It is her aim that Cloten should succeed to the throne – by fair means or foul. At this point Lucius, an ambassador from the Roman Emperor, has just politely asked for the tribute money that is owing to Rome. Cloten insists that the money should not be paid ('Britain's a world by itself, and we will nothing pay'). His mother then backs him up with this speech to her husband.

Although King Cymbeline really existed (generally called Cunobelius) around two thousand years ago, we know nothing about his real queen. She could be any age from early thirties to early fifties.

---

4   *As Neptune's park, ribbed and paled in* As if the sea ('Neptune's park') were fenced ('ribbed and paled')

5   *rocks* (This is 'oaks' or 'banks' in some editions.)

15   *Cassibelan* (Cymbeline's uncle – or, possibly, great-uncle.)

16   *to master* of mastering

      giglot fickle ('giglot' = loose woman)

17   *Lud's Town* London (Lud was Cymbeline's grandfather, and the town was supposed to have been named after him.)

Act 3, Scene 1
Queen –

1   Remember, sir, my liege,
        The kings your ancestors, together with
        The natural bravery of your isle, which stands
        As Neptune's park, ribbed and paled in
5   With rocks unscalable and roaring waters,
        With sands that will not bear your enemies' boats,
        But suck them up to th' topmast. A kind of conquest
        Caesar made here, but made not here his brag
        Of 'Came and saw and overcame'. With shame –
10   The first that ever touched him – he was carried
        From off our coast, twice beaten; and his shipping,
        Poor ignorant baubles, on our terrible seas
        Like eggshells moved upon their surges, cracked
        As easily 'gainst our rocks. For joy whereof
15   The famed Cassibelan, who was once at point –
        O giglot fortune! – to master Caesar's sword,
        Made Lud's Town with rejoicing fires bright,
18   And Britons strut with courage.

Hamlet

Ophelia

Ophelia is the daughter of Polonius (a councillor of state, close to Claudius, the King of Denmark), sister to Laertes and, before the play starts, loved by Hamlet. In her first scene she is gently warned by both her brother and father to be wary of Hamlet's approaches after what he's recently been through, i.e. the sudden death of his father (the recently deceased King) and its consequences for him. As the play progresses Hamlet's behaviour becomes more and more strange and irrational, culminating in him accidentally killing Polonius and hiding the body. Ophelia, deeply distracted by this event, suddenly appears before the Queen, and sings a strange song. Then the Queen asks her, 'Alas, sweet lady, what imports this song?'; this is Ophelia's response.

I have cut a few remarks of the King and Queen, and a few lines of Ophelia's to construct this speech.

Her earlier speeches, in Act 2, Scene 1 and Act 3, Scene 1, are quite often used for audition.

1	*Say you?* What do you say?
4–5	*At his head a grass-green turf, / At his heels a stone.* (These were traditional burial customs.)
8	*Larded* Adorned
9	*grave* (This is 'ground' in some editions.)
10	*true-love showers* loving tears
16	*betime* early
20	*dupped* opened
23	*la* (An exclamation emphasising 'Indeed'; this is not in some editions.)
	make an end on 't finish it (i.e. the song)
24	*Gis* Jesus
26	*do 't* (i.e. seduce young girls.)
27	*Cock* God (but also, penis.)
28	*tumbled me* made love to me (with some roughness)
30	*He answers* (This is not in some editions.)
31	*'a'* have (This is 'ha' in some editions.)
32	*An* If (This is 'And' in some editions.)

Act 4, Scene 5
Ophelia –

1   Say you? Nay, pray you, mark.
         [*sings*]   *He is dead and gone, lady,*
                       He is dead and gone.
                       At his head a grass-green turf,
5   *At his heels a stone.*
         Pray you, mark.
         [*sings*]   *White his shroud as the mountain snow –*
         [*Enter Claudius*]
                       Larded with sweet flowers,
                       Which bewept to the grave did – not – go
10   *With true-love showers.*
         They say the owl was a baker's daughter. Lord, we know
         what we are, but know not what we may be. God be at your
         table! Pray you, let's have no words of this, but when they
         ask you what it means, say you this:
15   [*sings*]   *Tomorrow is Saint Valentine's day,*
                       All in the morning betime,
                       And I a maid at your window
                       To be your Valentine.
                       Then up he rose, and donned his clothes,
20   *And dupped the chamber door;*
                       Let in the maid, that out a maid
                       Never departed more.
         Indeed, la? Without an oath, I'll make an end on 't.
         [*sings*]   *By Gis, and by Saint Charity,*
25   *Alack, and fie for shame!*
                       Young men will do 't if they come to 't,
                       By Cock, they are to blame.
                       Quoth she, 'Before you tumbled me,
                       You promised me to wed.'
30   He answers,
         [*sings*]   *'So would I 'a' done, by yonder sun,*
                       An thou hadst not come to my bed.'
         I hope all will be well. We must be patient. But I cannot
         choose but weep to think they should lay him i' th' cold
35   ground. My brother shall know of it. And so I thank you for
         your good counsel. Come, my coach! Good night, ladies,
37   good night, sweet ladies, good night, good night.   [*Exit*]

41

Henry IV, part 1

Lady Percy

Lady Elizabeth Percy, known as 'Kate' (1371–c.1444) is the wife of the fiery, gallant (sometimes vain, impulsive and foolish) Henry Percy (Hotspur). The Percy family had helped Henry IV seize the throne from Richard II, but they harbour a simmering resentment against Henry for his apparent ingratitude for that help. This resentment boils over through a series of disputes and pushes Hotspur to contemplate open rebellion. She has just walked in on him reading a letter and he has just said to her, 'How now, Kate? I must leave you within these two hours.' As the dialogue that follows this speech shows (and in Act 3, Scene 1), she is a spirited character and there generally seems to be a strong, sparky relationship between them.

The historical Lady Percy, and her husband, were much older than Shakespeare portrays them. At the time of this scene she would have been in her thirties; however, in the play, she comes over as someone in her late teens / early twenties.

Her speech beginning 'O yet, for God's sake, go not to these wars!' (in *Henry IV, part 2* – Act 2, Scene 3) is one of the most popular speeches on the audition circuit.

5	*stomach* appetite (for sex)
9	*given* given away
10	*thick-eyed* blind to others
	curst bad-tempered
13	*manège* horsemanship
15	*sallies* attacks
	retires retreats
16	*palisadoes* defensive works (constructed from iron-pointed stakes stuck in the ground)
	frontiers outworks (of a fortified position)
17	*basilisks* (The largest size of cannon.)
	cannon (Here, a medium-sized cannon.)
	culverin (The smallest size of cannon.)
18	*prisoners' ransom* (This is 'prisoners ransomed' in some editions.)
19	*currents* movements
	heady headstrong
23	*late* recently
24	*motions* emotions
26	*hest* command
27	*heavy* serious

Act 2, Scene 3 (Scene 4 in some editions)
Lady Percy –

Enter Lady Percy.

1   O my good lord, why are you thus alone?
For what offence have I this fortnight been
A banished woman from my Harry's bed?
Tell me, sweet lord, what is 't that takes from thee
5   Thy stomach, pleasure, and thy golden sleep?
Why dost thou bend thine eyes upon the earth,
And start so often when thou sit'st alone?
Why hast thou lost the fresh blood in thy cheeks,
And given my treasures and my rights of thee
10   To thick-eyed musing and curst melancholy?
In thy faint slumbers I by thee have watched,
And heard thee murmur tales of iron wars,
Speak terms of manège to thy bounding steed,
Cry 'Courage! To the field!' And thou hast talked
15   Of sallies and retires, of trenches, tents,
Of palisadoes, frontiers, parapets,
Of basilisks, of cannon, culverin,
Of prisoners' ransom, and of soldiers slain,
And all the currents of a heady fight.
20   Thy spirit within thee hath been so at war,
And thus hath so bestirred thee in thy sleep,
That beads of sweat have stood upon thy brow
Like bubbles in a late-disturbèd stream;
And in thy face strange motions have appeared,
25   Such as we see when men restrain their breath
On some great sudden hest. O, what portents are these?
Some heavy business hath my lord in hand,
28   And I must know it, else he loves me not.

Henry IV, part 2

Hostess Quickly

Hostess Quickly (also known as 'Hostess' and 'Mistress Quickly') is a widow and the hostess (mistress / proprietress) of the 'Boar's Head Tavern' in Eastcheap in the City of London. She is a warm-hearted woman who has known the famously fat and debauched Sir John Falstaff for 'these twenty-nine years'. She is very fond of him and he exploits this affection by borrowing money from her and neglects to pay it back. She has just summoned two officers, Fang and Snare, to arrest him for the debt. The officers hesitate, fearing for their own safety ('It may chance cost some of us our lives, for he will stab'), and she interrupts with this outburst. In her verbosity she often gets her words confused. She could be any age from thirty upwards.

All the locations mentioned are within about half a mile of each other.

1	*going* (i.e. to the wars – without repaying his debt to her.)
	warrant assure
1–2	*infinitive thing* huge drain (She means 'infinite' rather than 'infinitive'.)
2	*upon my score* on my finances
	sure securely
3	*'A* He
	continuantly continually
4	*Pie Corner* (At a corner of the old Smithfield Market in the City of London – known for its cook-shops, where pigs were killed, cooked and made into pies.)
	saving your manhoods no offence intended (It's probable that Pie Corner was also a haunt of prostitutes.)
	a saddle (There were also saddlers in the area, but she may also be implying 'that which is mounted' – a prostitute.)
5	*indited* invited
	Lubber's Head (An inn.)
5–6	*Lombard Street* (This is 'Lumbert Street' in some editions.)
7	*exion is entered* lawsuit has begun
8	*mark* two-thirds of a pound (100 marks would be equivalent to over a thousand pounds today.)
8–9	*long one* large amount
10&11	*fobbed* put (This is 'fubbed' in some editions.)
15	*arrant* notorious
	malmsey-nose red-nosed (Malmsey is a strong, sweet red wine.)
17	*do me* do for me
	offices duties (as officers of the law)

Act 2, Scene 1
Hostess Quickly –

1   I am undone by his going, I warrant you; he's an infinitive thing upon my score. Good Master Fang, hold him sure. Good Master Snare, let him not 'scape. 'A comes continuantly to Pie Corner – saving your manhoods – to buy a saddle; and

5   he is indited to dinner to the Lubber's Head in Lombard Street, to Master Smooth's the silkman. I pray you, since my exion is entered, and my case so openly known to the world, let him be brought in to his answer. A hundred mark is a long one for a poor lone woman to bear; and I have borne, and

10   borne, and borne, and have been fobbed off, and fobbed off, and fobbed off, from this day to that day, that it is a shame to be thought on. There is no honesty in such dealing, unless a woman should be made an ass and a beast, to bear every knave's wrong.

Enter Sir John Falstaff, Bardolph, and the Page

15   Yonder he comes, and that arrant malmsey-nose knave Bardolph with him. Do your offices, do your offices, Master

17   Fang and Master Snare; do me, do me, do me your offices.

Henry IV, part 2

Hostess Quickly

Hostess Quickly (also known as 'Hostess' and 'Mistress Quickly') is a widow and the hostess (mistress / proprietress) of the 'Boar's Head Tavern' in Eastcheap in the City of London. She is a warm-hearted woman who has known the famously fat and debauched Sir John Falstaff for 'these twenty-nine years'. She is very fond of him and he exploits this affection by borrowing money from her and neglects to pay it back. She has summoned two officers, Fang and Snare, to arrest him for the debt. Falstaff, accompanied by Bardolph and the page, has just appeared and there is nearly a fight which is stopped by the arrival of the Lord Chief Justice and his men. The Justice insists Falstaff repays her. He asks her, 'What is the gross sum that I owe thee?' This is her response.

In her verbosity she often gets her words confused. She could be any age from thirty upwards.

---

1   *Marry* Why, to be sure (A mild swear-word literally meaning, 'by the Virgin Mary'.)
2   *parcel-gilt* partially gilded (usually on the inner surface of silver bowls, cups, etc.)
3   *Dolphin chamber* (Inn-rooms had, and sometimes still have, fanciful names.)
       sea-coal (i.e. mineral coal, brought to London by sea from Newcastle, as distinct from charcoal.)
4   *Wheeson* Whitsun
5   *liking* likening
       singing-man of Windsor (i.e. someone with a trivial-seeming job.)
7   *my lady* (i.e. the wife of a knight.)
9   *Gossip* Neighbour (a friendly term of address)
       mess small amount
10   *whereby* whereupon
12   *green* unhealed
13   *familiarity* familiar
15   *madam* (A knight's wife was entitled to be called 'madam'.)
16   *thirty shillings* (i.e. several hundred pounds in modern terms.)
       book-oath oath on the Bible

Act 2, Scene 1
Hostess Quickly –

1   Marry, if thou wert an honest man, thyself, and the money too. Thou didst swear to me upon a parcel-gilt goblet, sitting in my Dolphin chamber, at the round table, by a sea-coal fire, upon Wednesday in Wheeson week, when the Prince broke

5   thy head for liking his father to a singing-man of Windsor – thou didst swear to me then, as I was washing thy wound, to marry me, and make me my lady thy wife. Canst thou deny it? Did not goodwife Keech, the butcher's wife, come in then, and call me 'Gossip Quickly'? – coming in to borrow a mess

10   of vinegar, telling us she had a good dish of prawns, whereby thou didst desire to eat some, whereby I told thee they were ill for a green wound? And didst thou not, when she was gone downstairs, desire me to be no more so familiarity with such poor people, saying that ere long they should call me

15   'madam'? And didst thou not kiss me, and bid me fetch thee thirty shillings? I put thee now to thy book-oath. Deny it if

17   thou canst. [*She weeps*]

Henry VIII

Katherine of Aragon

Katherine of Aragon, Queen of England (1485–1536) was the first wife of Henry VIII. She only had one surviving child (Mary) and after twenty years of marriage, Henry, desperate for a male heir and with an eye for Anne Boleyn, institutes divorce proceedings based on a disputed reading of catholic church law. She refuses to accept the idea and here Cardinals Wolsey and Campeius are trying to get her to change her mind. The Cardinals have been gently trying to persuade her and she becomes more angry, and Campeius has just said, 'Your rage mistakes us' (i.e. 'In your anger you are misjudging us').

Although she was Spanish by birth, she had lived in England for most of her adult life, so she could have a slight accent. She was forty-three at the time.

In the play Wolsey speaks between lines 10 and 11.

Her wonderful courtroom speeches (Act 2, Scene 4) are very often used in audition.

2	*cardinal virtues* (These were 'justice, prudence, temperance and fortitude'; the theological virtues, 'faith, hope, and charity' were added to mirror the seven deadly sins. She is also punning, in that she is talking to two Cardinals.)
3	*cardinal sins* (She continues the pun with a reference to the seven deadly sins.)
4	*Mend* Reform
5	*cordial* comfort
6	*lost* brought to ruin
9	*at once* one day
11	*turn me into nothing* won't change ('turn') my mind
12	*false professors* (The Cardinals have been using scholarly theological arguments to justify the divorce.)
14	*anything but churchmen's habits* anything more than your official robes
16	*he's* (This is 'has' in some editions.)
17	*old* (She is forty-three, but life-expectancy at that time was only about forty (perhaps higher for the well-fed aristocracy) and she's been through enough emotional trauma to age anyone.)
18	*fellowship* contact
20	*above* on top of
21	*Make me accursed* Bring me misery ('accursed' is 'a curse' in some editions.)

Act 3, Scene 1
Queen Katherine –

1   The more shame for ye! Holy men I thought ye,
Upon my soul, two reverend cardinal virtues;
But cardinal sins and hollow hearts I fear ye.
Mend 'em, for shame, my lords! Is this your comfort?
5   The cordial that ye bring a wretched lady,
A woman lost among ye, laughed at, scorned?
I will not wish ye half my miseries;
I have more charity. But say I warned ye.
Take heed, for heaven's sake take heed, lest at once
10   The burden of my sorrows fall upon ye.
Ye turn me into nothing. Woe upon ye,
And all such false professors. Would you have me –
If you have any justice, any pity,
If ye be anything but churchmen's habits –
15   Put my sick cause into his hands that hates me?
Alas, he's banished me his bed already;
His love, too, long ago. I am old, my lords,
And all the fellowship I hold now with him
Is only my obedience. What can happen
20   To me above this wretchedness? All your studies
21   Make me accursed like this.

Henry VIII

Katherine of Aragon

Katherine of Aragon, Queen of England (1485–1536) was the first wife of Henry VIII. She only had one surviving child (Mary) and after twenty years of marriage, Henry, desperate for a male heir and with an eye for Anne Boleyn, divorced her. She never accepted this (it was based on disputed reading of catholic church law); nevertheless, Henry allowed her to live out her life in some comfort. This is from her last scene of the play and she is giving her instructions to Capuchius (an ambassador from Rome and her nephew), who has been sent (too late) by Henry to wish her better health. She has just given him her last letter to Henry which he has agreed to deliver.

Although she was Spanish by birth, she had lived in England for most of her adult life, so she could have a slight accent. She was forty-three at the time.

Her wonderful courtroom speeches (Act 2, Scene 4) are very often used in audition.

3	*long trouble* (i.e. her resistance to the idea of divorce.)
6	*Griffith* (Her gentleman-usher and something of a confidante.)
	Patience (Her waiting-woman.)
10	*maiden flowers* (Flowers symbolising chastity – e.g. daffodils, violets, primroses, and so on.)
11	*lay me forth* lay me out for burial
12	*daughter to a king* (Her father was King Ferdinand of Spain.)

Act 4, Scene 2
Queen Katherine –

1   I thank you, honest lord. Remember me
In all humility unto his highness.
Say his long trouble now is passing
Out of this world. Tell him, in death I blessed him,
5   For so I will. Mine eyes grow dim. Farewell,
My lord. Griffith, farewell. [*To her woman*] Nay, Patience,
You must not leave me yet. I must to bed.
Call in more women. When I am dead, good wench,
Let me be used with honour; strew me over
10   With maiden flowers, that all the world may know
I was a chaste wife to my grave. Embalm me,
Then lay me forth. Although unqueened, yet like
A queen and daughter to a king, inter me.
14   I can no more.

> *Exeunt Capuchius and Griffith at one door;*
> *Patience leading Katherine at another*

King John

Blanche

Blanche of Spain (1188–1252) was a niece to King John. Her marriage to Lewis, the French Dauphin, was arranged as part of an alliance with King Philip of France, Lewis' father. In later life Blanche became quite a considerable force in French history. Her husband died young and she acted as regent for her son and ruled very effectively whilst he grew up and later when he was away fighting in the Crusades. At this point in the play, she and Lewis have just been married but the celebrations have been interrupted by Cardinal Pandulph, an emissary from the Pope. He demands that King John give way in a dispute over the archbishopric of Canterbury. John will not give way so Pandulph excommunicates him and demands that Philip break the new alliance and make war on John. Philip eventually agrees, encouraged by Lewis. This speech is Blanche's attempt to change the minds of the two factions – both of whom is she is now closely related to. Historically, she was in her early teens at this time.

This is several speeches put together and, in the play, King Philip finally decides to declare war on King John about half way through this speech. However, I have adapted a line of Lewis' for her use and made a few other minor modifications to make it a longer plea for peace.

2	*blood* (i.e. King John and his family.)
4	*churlish* grudging
5	*measures to our pomp* the music of our wedding celebrations
15	*dismember* (A form of execution in which the condemned were torn apart by their arms and legs being tied to horses which were then driven in opposite directions.)
18	*Father* (King Philip, her father-in-law)
	fortune victory
19	*Grandam* Grandmother (Eleanor of Aquitaine, also mother of King John and very much in favour of going to war.)

Act 3, Scene 1
Blanche –

1   Husband, to arms? Upon thy wedding day?
    Against the blood that thou hast marrièd?
    What, shall our feast be kept with slaughtered men?
    Shall braying trumpets and loud churlish drums,
5   Clamours of hell, be measures to our pomp?
    O husband, hear me! Ay, alack, how new
    Is 'husband' in my mouth! Even for that name
    Which till this time my tongue did ne'er pronounce,
    Upon my knee I beg, go not to arms
10   Against mine uncle. O, what motive may
    Be stronger with thee than the name of wife?
    Which is the side that I must go withal?
    I am with both; each army hath a hand,
    And in their rage, I having hold of both,
15   They whirl asunder and dismember me.
    Husband, I cannot pray that thou mayst win;
    Uncle, I needs must pray that thou mayst lose.
    Father, I may not wish the fortune thine;
    Grandam, I will not wish thy wishes thrive.
20   Whoever wins, on that side shall I lose –
21   Assurèd loss before the match be played.

King Lear

Cordelia

Cordelia is King Lear's youngest and most honest daughter, whom he mistakenly rejects. In the first scene of the play, knowing she will marry, Cordelia refuses to assert that all of her love will forever go to her father (as he demands) – unlike Regan and Goneril, her hypocritical sisters. Lear mistakes Cordelia's honesty for a lack of affection and disinherits her. She marries the King of France and is not seen again until this scene, when she arrives with an army to help her father recover his throne. She has just heard that her once proud father is in a desperate physical and mental state.

There is more than one viable version of this play-text. The Folio is the most authoritative one, but the Quarto edition contains some extra lines (and detailed variations) that are now generally incorporated into the published versions of the play.

This is such a famous play that it is important that you are prepared to justify the performance decisions you make with this speech.

I have cut lines of the Doctor, a Messenger and Cordelia to construct this speech.

---

	with drum and colours with drums beating and flags waving (which indicates readiness for battle)
1	*he* (i.e. Lear)
3	*rank* evil-smelling
3-5	*fumitor... Darnel* (These are all weeds of bitter, pungent, or poisonous kinds. 'Fumitor' is 'fumiter' or 'femiter' in some editions.)
5	*idle* worthless (as opposed to 'sustaining corn', which is the staff of life)
6	*century* a hundred soldiers
7	*high-grown* overgrown
8	*What can man's wisdom* What can man's ingenuity do
9	*In the restoring* To restore
11	*virtues of the earth* health-restoring medicinal plants (and people)
12	*Spring* Arise (as herbs do after a spring shower)
	aidant and remediate helpful and curative
15	*That wants the means* That lacks the sanity
16	*thy business* your cause
17	*blown* inflated
18	*ag'd* aged

Act 4, Scene 4
(Scene 3 in some editions; Scene 18 in the Quarto edition)
Cordelia –

Enter with drum and colours, Cordelia, Doctor, and soldiers

1   Alack, 'tis he! Why, he was met even now
As mad as the vexed sea, singing aloud,
Crowned with rank fumitor and furrow-weeds,
With burdocks, hemlock, nettles, cuckoo-flowers,
5   Darnel, and all the idle weeds that grow
In our sustaining corn. [*To soldiers*] A century send forth.
Search every acre in the high-grown field,
And bring him to our eye.   [*Exeunt soldiers*]
                                        What can man's wisdom
In the restoring his bereavèd sense?
10 He that helps him, take all my outward worth.
All you unpublished virtues of the earth,
Spring with my tears, be aidant and remediate
In the good man's distress! – Seek, seek for him,
Lest his ungoverned rage dissolve the life
15 That wants the means to lead it. – Dear father,
It is thy business that I go about.
No blown ambition doth our arms incite,
But love, dear love, and our ag'd father's right.
19 Soon may I hear and see him!   *Exeunt*

Love's Labours Lost

The Princess of France

The Princess of France (we're never given a first name) is a very sharp, witty and straight-forward lady. Technically, she is on a diplomatic mission to the King of Navarre (now part in France and part in Spain) with her three attendant ladies. In this speech (her first of the play) she is responding to Boyet, an attendant Lord, who has just been very flattering to her. He (and the ladies) are very much her friends and she rarely pulls rank. She could be as young as late teens.

1	*but mean* not great
2	*painted flourish* over the top-ness
3	*bought by judgement* through serious consideration
4	*base sale of chapmen's tongues.* a salesman's pitch. (Chapmen were hawkers or pedlars.)
8	*task the tasker* (She's implying that she's now really going to get at him, but she softens to give him a specific 'task' that is important to her and her ladies.)
9	*fame* rumour
11	*painful* diligent
	shall outwear is sustained for
13	*to 's* to us
16	*Bold* Confident
17	*best-moving fair solicitor* most elegantly persuasive on our behalf
20	*Importunes* Asks for

Act 2, Scene 1
Princess –

*The park. Enter the Princess of France with three attending
ladies – Maria, Katherine, and Rosaline – and a lord named
Boyet*

1   Good Lord Boyet, my beauty, though but mean,
     Needs not the painted flourish of your praise.
     Beauty is bought by judgement of the eye,
     Not uttered by base sale of chapmen's tongues.
5   I am less proud to hear you tell my worth
     Than you much willing to be counted wise
     In spending your wit in the praise of mine.
     But now to task the tasker: good Boyet,
     You are not ignorant, all-telling fame
10   Doth noise abroad Navarre hath made a vow,
     Till painful study shall outwear three years,
     No woman may approach his silent court.
     Therefore to 's seemeth it a needful course,
     Before we enter his forbidden gates,
15   To know his pleasure; and in that behalf,
     Bold of your worthiness, we single you
     As our best-moving fair solicitor.
     Tell him the daughter of the King of France,
     On serious business, craving quick dispatch,
20   Importunes personal conference with his grace.
     Haste, signify so much, while we attend,
22   Like humble-visaged suitors, his high will.

Love's Labours Lost

The Princess of France

The Princess of France (we're never given a first name) is a very sharp, witty and straight-forward lady. Technically, she is on a diplomatic mission to the King of Navarre (now part in France and part in Spain) with her three attendant ladies. 'Diplomacy' turns to fun and much of the play is spent in verbal flirtations and battles of wits between her and her ladies and the King and his attendant lords. At this point she has just arrived for a deer hunt (probably with crossbows) with her ladies (Rosaline, Maria, and Katherine), Boyet (an attendant lord) and a forester. She could be as young as late teens.

I have changed one word and cut lines of the Forester and Boyet to construct this speech.

2	*steep uprising* (This is 'steep-up rising' in some editions.)
3	*'a* he
	mounting mind (There is a hint of sexual innuendo here.)
5	*On* (This is 'Ere' in some editions.)
7	*murderer* (This is 'murtherer' in some editions.)
8	*mercy* (i.e. her merciful self.)
9	*then* consequently (i.e. when it is a merciful person, like me, who is doing the shooting.)
11	*Not wounding* Not by wounding
14	*out of question* without doubt
15	*Glory* Desire for glory
	detested detestable
17	*bend to that* corrupt

Act 4, Scene 1
Princess –

1   Was that the King that spurred his horse so ha
       Against the steep uprising of the hill?
       Whoe'er 'a was, 'a showed a mounting mind.
       Well, lords, today we shall have our dispatch.
5   On Saturday we will return to France.
       Then, forester my friend, where is the bush
       That we must stand and play the murderer in?
       Then come, the bow. Now mercy goes to kill,
       And shooting well is then accounted ill.
10   Thus will I save my credit in the shoot:
       Not wounding, pity would not let me do 't;
       If wounding, then it was to show my skill,
       That more for praise than purpose meant to kill.
       And, out of question, so it is sometimes:
15   Glory grows guilty of detested crimes
       When for fame's sake, for praise, an outward part,
       We bend to that the working of the heart;
       As I for praise alone now seek to spill
19   The poor deer's blood that my heart means no ill.

The Merchant of Venice

Nerissa

Nerissa is lady-in-waiting and confidante to Portia, a rich heiress. Throughout the play she is a pert and lively companion to her mistress. This is the first time we see them and Portia has just said, 'By my troth, Nerissa, my little body is aweary of this great world' and then there is dialogue about Portia's feelings on having a husband chosen through the famous caskets. Although it is somewhat cheeky of me to turn this into a monologue (and add the word 'weary'), I think it is perfectly reasonable to turn Portia's 'weariness' into silence and imagine Nerissa trying to cheer her up by reviewing the whole situation. She is probably in her late-teens or early twenties, but could be up to late thirties.

I have slightly changed the punctuation and taken a few words of Portia's to construct this speech.

3	*surfeit* go to excess (usually in eating and drinking)
5	*in the mean* in the middle
	Superfluity Excessiveness
6	*competency* moderation
14	*County* Count
	by concerning
21–22	*by some other sort* in some other manner
22	*imposition* will

Act 1, Scene 2
Nerissa –

1   You would be weary, sweet madam, if your miseries were in
     the same abundance as your good fortunes are; and yet, for
     aught I see, they are as sick that surfeit with too much as they
     that starve with nothing. It is no mean happiness, therefore,
5   to be seated in the mean. Superfluity comes sooner by white
     hairs, but competency lives longer. Your father was ever
     virtuous, and holy men at their death have good inspirations;
     therefore the lottery that he hath devised in these three chests
     of gold, silver, and lead, whereof who chooses his meaning
10   chooses you, will no doubt never be chosen by any rightly
     but one who you shall rightly love. But what warmth is there
     in your affection towards any of these princely suitors that
     are already come? First there is the Neapolitan prince, then is
     there the County Palatine. How say you by the French lord,
15   Monsieur le Bon? What say you then to Falconbridge, the
     young baron of England? What think you of the Scottish lord,
     his neighbour? How like you the young German, the Duke of
     Saxony's nephew? You need not fear, lady, the having any of
     these lords. They have acquainted me with their deter-
20   minations, which is indeed to return to their home and to
     trouble you with no more suit, unless you may be won by
     some other sort than your father's imposition depending on
     the caskets. Do you not remember, lady, in your father's time,
     a Venetian, a scholar and a soldier, that came hither in
25   company of the Marquis of Montferrat? It was Bassanio – as
     I think, so was he called. He of all the men that ever my
27   foolish eyes looked upon was the best deserving a fair lady.

The Merchant of Venice

Jessica

Jessica is the daughter of Shylock, the Jewish money-lender, and beloved of Lorenzo, a Christian. She is an apparently straight-forward and lively young woman, but she abandons her father and her religion when she elopes with Lorenzo, and she also steals Shylock's money. In Shakespeare's time her actions would have been largely justified in the prevailing anti-Semitic climate. Money-lending was strictly against the Christian ethic, so the job fell to the Jewish 'outcasts', which consequently served to make them hated. However, Shylock does generate some sympathy. In playing Jessica now, I think it is important to take on board (at least to some extent) the enormity of what she is actually doing – it can't entirely be a completely spontaneous decision.

This is her first appearance in the play, and Lancelot (spelled 'Launcelot' in many editions), a servant to Shylock, has not long before described his angst over his decision whether to leave his master for Bassanio, also a Christian.

I have cut Lancelot's speech that comes in the middle of line 9 and cut a word to restore the meter.

4	*ducat* (Gold (or silver) coins, then, worth about 50p, i.e. probably equivalent to at least ten pounds in modern terms; the silver ones were about a third of this value.)
5	*soon at supper* at supper early this evening
9	(Some editions put Lancelot's exit after 'talk with thee.')
13	*manners* beliefs and behaviours
14	*strife* (i.e. within herself over leaving her father and her religion.)

Act 2, Scene 3
Jessica –

Enter Jessica and Lancelot, the clown

1   I am sorry thou wilt leave my father so.
    Our house is hell; and thou, a merry devil,
    Didst rob it of some taste of tediousness.
    But fare thee well. There is a ducat for thee.
5   And, Lancelot, soon at supper shalt thou see
    Lorenzo, who is thy new master's guest.
    Give him this letter; do it secretly.
    And so farewell. I would not have my father
    See me talk with thee. Farewell, good Lancelot.

                                        Exit Lancelot

10 Alack, what heinous sin is it in me
    To be ashamed to be my father's child.
    But though I am a daughter to his blood,
    I am not to his manners. O Lorenzo,
    If thou keep promise, I shall end this strife,
15 Become a Christian and thy loving wife.   *Exit*

The Merry Wives of Windsor

Mistress (Margaret) Page

Mistress (Margaret) Page is the Elizabethan equivalent of a suburban housewife, happily married to the mild and cheerful George, and mother to Anne and William. She hardly knows the famously fat and debauched Sir John Falstaff ('he hath not been thrice in my company'), but she has just received this love letter from him. She is generally a good humoured and charming lady. Although she is generally played in her forties, she could be as young as thirty.

1	*'scaped* escaped
	holiday-time hey-day
4–5	*for though Love use Reason for his precisian, he admits him not for his counsellor.* (Falstaff is telling her not to be concerned that 'Reason' might (morally) be against their liaison; a 'precisian' was an austere adviser in spiritual matters.)
6	*sympathy* agreement (between us)
7	*sack* (A Spanish wine; usually white.)
18	*Herod of Jewry* (i.e. an audacious villain. Herod ordered the Slaughter of the Innocents in his attempt to kill the infant Christ.)
20	*unweighed* thoughtless
21	*Flemish* (The inhabitants of the Low Countries were renowned for their drunkenness.)
	i' th' (This is 'with the' in some editions.)
22	*conversation* behaviour
	assay assail
23	*should I say* can I have said
25	*exhibit* propose
26	*O God, that I knew how to* (This is 'How shall I be' in some editions.)
27	*puddings* sausages

Act 2, Scene 1
Mistress Page –

Before Page's House. Enter Mistress Page, with a letter

1 What, have I 'scaped love-letters in the holiday-time of my beauty, and am I now a subject for them? Let me see.
[*She reads*]

Ask me no reason why I love you, for though Love use Reason for
5 *his precisian, he admits him not for his counsellor. You are not young; no more am I. Go to, then, there's sympathy. You are merry; so am I. Ha, ha, then, there's more sympathy. You love sack, and so do I. Would you desire better sympathy? Let it suffice thee, Mistress Page, at the least if the love of soldier can suffice, that I*
10 *love thee. I will not say 'pity me' – 'tis not a soldier-like phrase – but I say, 'love me'. By me,*

> *Thine own true knight,*
> *By day or night*
> *Or any kind of light,*
15 > *With all his might*
> *For thee to fight,*

> *John Falstaff.*

What a Herod of Jewry is this! O, wicked, wicked world! One that is well-nigh worn to pieces with age, to show himself a
20 young gallant! What an unweighed behaviour hath this Flemish drunkard picked, i' th' devil's name, out of my conversation, that he dares in this manner assay me? Why, he hath not been thrice in my company. What should I say to him? I was then frugal of my mirth, heaven forgive me. Why,
25 I'll exhibit a bill in the Parliament for the putting down of men. O God, that I knew how to be revenged on him! For
27 revenged I will be, as sure as his guts are made of puddings.

The Merry Wives of Windsor

Mistress Quickly

Mistress Quickly is similar to but not the same as Hostess Quickly in *Henry IV* and *Henry V*. In this play she is 'nurse, or his dry nurse, or his cook, or his laundry, his washer and his wringer' and unknown to Falstaff at the beginning. However, she is similarly shrewd and comic, and very happy to meddle in other people's affairs, as her counterpart in the history plays. She also has a happy knack of (innocently) getting her words wrong and of sometimes making up completely new ones. Although she is generally played older, she could be as young as mid-twenties.

Sir John Falstaff has written love letters to two respectable, middle-class housewives – Mistress Ford and Mistress Page. The two women are at first confused and then furious when they discover that their letters are exactly the same. They plan a revenge and first decide to lead Falstaff into believing that they are both interested in him. Mistress Quickly agrees to be the go-between and meets up with Falstaff. After some opening banter he enquires about Mistress Ford and this is her response.

1	*Marry* Why, to be sure (A mild swear-word literally meaning, 'By the Virgin Mary'.)
2	*canaries* state of confusion ('Canary' is the name of an energetic Spanish dance and of a light sweet wine from the Canary Islands. Also 'canary' in line 4.)
3	*lay* was in residence
7	*musk* (A strong perfume.)
	rushling rustling (Some editions have 'rustling', but I enjoy Quickly's misuse of words.)
8	*alligant* elegant or eloquent
10	*eye-wink* glance
11 & 12	*angels* gold coins (i.e. as a bribe to gain access to Mistress Ford.)
12	*defy* reject
	in any such sort of any kind
15	*pensioners* gentlemen of the royal bodyguard (However, they would not be superior to earls; she is becoming even more confused.)

Act 2, Scene 2
Mistress Quickly –

1   Marry, this is the short and the long of it. You have brought
     her into such a canaries as 'tis wonderful. The best courtier of
     them all, when the court lay at Windsor, could never have
     brought her to such a canary. Yet there has been knights, and
5   lords, and gentlemen, with their coaches – I warrant you,
     coach after coach, letter after letter, gift after gift – smelling so
     sweetly, all musk; and so rushling, I warrant you, in silk and
     gold, and in such alligant terms, and in such wine and sugar
     of the best and the fairest, that would have won any woman's
10   heart; and, I warrant you, they could never get an eye-wink
     of her. I had myself twenty angels given me this morning –
     but I defy all angels, in any such sort, as they say, but in the
     way of honesty. And, I warrant you, they could never get her
     so much as sip on a cup with the proudest of them all. And
15   yet there has been earls, nay, which is more, pensioners. But,
16   I warrant you, all is one with her.

Much Ado About Nothing

Hero

Hero is the daughter of Leonato, the governor of Messina. On the surface she is a well brought up young lady. However, she is perfectly capable – as in this scene – of having fun. She is with one of her gentlewomen, Ursula – who is her close friend whilst also being her servant. Everybody knows that Hero's cousin Beatrice is madly in love with Benedick (and vice-versa), but neither will admit it to the other. Hero has organised a ploy to trick Beatrice into following her true feelings. She has sent her other servant, Margaret, to tell Beatrice that Hero and Ursula are talking about her in the orchard. Beatrice has swallowed the bait and is hiding and overhearing them – something that Hero and Ursula are very well aware of. She could be any age between mid-teens and early twenties.

I have made minor word changes to compensate for cutting Ursula's lines.

The ladies are having huge fun, but it is important that in all this the content sounds sincere to the listening Beatrice.

1	*he* (i.e. Benedick.)
6	*Misprising* Despising
8	*All matter else* All other conversation
9	*project* idea
10	*self-endeared* in love with herself
11	*How* However
	rarely wonderfully
12	*spell him backward* malign him (Line 19 is another way of saying this.)
14	*black* swarthy
	antic grotesque figure
16	*agate* (A stone commonly set into rings and, in which, small human figures were cut. This is 'agot' in some editions.)
21	*simpleness* integrity
	purchaseth deserve
22	*from* against
26	*press me to death* ('Pressing' was a punishment for those who refused to plead neither guilty or not guilty – heavy weights were placed on the accused's chest until they either pleaded or died.)
27	*covered fire* (i.e. banked up to burn slowly.)
29 & 30	*with* from

Act 3, Scene 1
Hero –

1   O god of love! I know he doth deserve
       As much as may be yielded to a man.
       But nature never framed a woman's heart
       Of prouder stuff than that of Beatrice.
5   Disdain and scorn ride sparkling in her eyes,
       Misprising what they look on; and her wit
       Values itself so highly that to her
       All matter else seems weak. She cannot love,
       Nor take no shape nor project of affection,
10   She is so self-endeared. I ne'er saw man,
       How wise, how noble, young, how rarely featured,
       But she would spell him backward. If fair-faced,
       She would swear the gentleman should be her sister;
       If black, why nature, drawing of an antic,
15   Made a foul blot; if tall, a lance ill-headed;
       If low, an agate very vilely cut;
       If speaking, why, a vane blown with all winds;
       If silent, why, a block movèd with none.
       So turns she every man the wrong side out,
20   And never gives to truth and virtue that
       Which simpleness and merit purchaseth.
       Sure, not to be so odd and from all fashions,
       As Beatrice is, cannot be commendable.
       But who dare tell her so? If I should speak
25   She would mock me into air; O, she would laugh me
       Out of myself, press me to death with wit.
       Therefore let Benedick, like covered fire,
       Consume away in sighs, waste inwardly.
       It were a better death than die with mocks,
30   Which is as bad as die with tickling.

Much Ado About Nothing

Margaret

Margaret is a gentlewoman attending Hero, cousin to Beatrice. We only see her in scenes full of fun, to which she is a significant contributor – Benedick says her 'wit is as quick as the greyhound's mouth'.

Everybody knows that Hero's cousin Beatrice is madly in love with Benedick (and vice-versa), but neither will admit it to the other. In this scene Margaret, Hero and Ursula (another gentlewoman) are sending Beatrice up about Benedick. Beatrice has just challenged an insinuation of Margaret's and this is Margaret's response. She is probably in her late-teens or early twenties, but could be up to late thirties.

This speech may look short but it is perfectly adequate for an audition.

1–2	*meant plain* literally meant
2	*holy-thistle* the blessed thistle (This was supposed to prevent disease.)
3	*by'r Lady* by Our Lady (i.e. Mary, mother of Christ.)
4	*list* please
7	*Yet* Previously
	such another behaved the same as you
9	*eats his meat without grudging* (i.e. is content.)
10	*converted* (i.e. into the idea of falling in love.)

Act 3, Scene 4
Margaret –

1   Moral? No, by my troth, I have no moral mean
       plain holy-thistle. You may think, perchance, that   ou
       are in love. Nay, by'r Lady, I am not such a fool to think what
       I list; nor I list not to think what I can; nor, indeed, I cannot
5   think, if I would think my heart out of thinking, that you are
       in love, or that you will be in love, or that you can be in love.
       Yet Benedick was such another, and now is he become a man;
       he swore he would never marry, and yet now, in despite of
       his heart, he eats his meat without grudging. And how you
10   may be converted I know not; but methinks you look with
11   your eyes as other women do.

Othello

Emilia

Emilia is the wife of Iago (an aide to Othello) and lady-in-waiting (and confidante) to Desdemona, wife of Othello. She is a sharp-tongued, worldly-wise woman who sticks by Iago in spite of his insults. He even accuses her of sleeping with Othello.

After a happy start to Othello and Desdemona's marriage, Othello starts to believe that she is sleeping with another of his aides (Cassio) and has not long before this speech suggested that she is a 'whore'. (Unknown to Emilia, all of this is a slander has been spread by Iago, who is jealous of Cassio's promotion.) Emilia and Iago enter to find Desdemona in a somewhat dazed state. Emilia is completely loyal to Desdemona and when Iago (feigning innocence) asks about what's been happening, Emilia tells him of Othello's accusation and then responds to Iago's, 'How comes this trick upon him?' with this tirade. She is probably in her twenties but could be older.

I have cut brief lines of Desdemona and Iago to construct this speech.

Her speech (at the end of Act 4, Scene 3) starting, 'Yes a dozen...' is very often used for audition.

2	*busy* meddling
	insinuating devious
3	*cogging* cheating
	cozening deceiving
	to get some office to get promotion
5	*halter* hangman's rope
7	*form* appearance
8 & 16	*the Moor* (i.e. Othello.)
8	*villainous* (This is 'outrageous' in some editions.)
10	*companions* (i.e. hangers-on.)
	thou'dst you would
	unfold reveal
14	*squire* (Literally, a knight's attendant, but she's using it derogatorily, in the sense of someone of low rank.)
15	*the seamy side without* inside out (i.e. made you suspicious and cynical.)
16	*made you to suspect me with the Moor* (In Act 1, Scene 3 Iago says that there are rumours of Othello having slept with Emilia.)

Act 4, Scene 2
Emilia –

1   I will be hanged if some eternal villain,
        Some busy and insinuating rogue,
        Some cogging, cozening slave, to get some office,
        Have not devised this slander; I'll be hanged else.
5   A halter pardon him, and hell gnaw his bones!
        Why should he call her whore? Who keeps her company?
        What place, what time, what form, what likelihood?
        The Moor's abused by some most villainous knave,
        Some base, notorious knave, some scurvy fellow.
10   O heaven, that such companions thou'dst unfold,
        And put in every honest hand a whip
        To lash the rascals naked through the world,
        Even from the east to the west!
        O, fie upon them! Some such squire he was
15   That turned your wit the seamy side without,
16   And made you to suspect me with the Moor.

Pericles

Thaisa

Thaisa is the daughter of King Simonides of Pentapolis. She is wooed by six knights. The King arranges a tournament to decide who shall marry her, which is won by Pericles, Prince of Tyre. However, because of his shabby appearance (after being shipwrecked in Pentapolis), he is derided by the others and Simonides says of his daughter, 'for this twelvemonth she'll not undertake / A married life.' The knights, apart from Pericles, leave. Simonides then reveals that he has a letter from his daughter in which she writes that, 'she'll wed the stranger knight / Or never more to view nor day nor night.' This pleases Simonides, but he decides to 'dissemble' (disguise his real feelings) in front of Pericles and Thaisa in order to test the young man. The King shows Pericles the letter and accuses him of bewitching his daughter, then she appears and Pericles asks her to 'Resolve your angry father if my tongue / Did e'er solicit, or my hand subscribe / To any syllable made love to you.' This is her response.

She is probably in her late teens or early twenties.

This is three speeches edited together and most editions only contain the first two lines.

3	*base* (i.e. of humble origin.)
	when that his life when his demeanour (and actions)
5	*ground* basis
6	*Enough* All this is enough
13	*being* (i.e. point to my existence.)
	joying of delighting in

74

Act 2, Scene 5 (Scene 9 in some editions)
Thaisa –

1   *[to Pericles]* Why, sir, say if you had,
        Who takes offence at that would make me glad?
        [kneeling to Simonides]
        Suppose his birth were base, when that his life
        Shows that he is not so; yet he hath virtue,
5   The very ground of all nobility,
        Enough to make him noble. I entreat you
        To remember that I am in love,
        The power of which love cannot be confined
        By th' power of your will. Most royal father,
10   What with my pen I have in secret written
        With my tongue now I openly confirm,
        Which is I have no life but in his love,
        Nor any being but in joying of his worth.
        [to Pericles] For every drop of blood he sheds of yours
15   He'll draw another from his only child.

Pericles

Dionyza

Dionyza is the wife of Cleon, Governor of Tharsus. Earlier in the play Pericles (thinking that his own wife, Thaisa, is dead) has left his infant daughter, Marina, in their care. As Marina grows she over-shadows Dionyza's own daughter. The jealous foster-mother has forced her servant Leonine to swear to kill Marina. At this point she is trying to persuade Marina to go for a healthy walk with Leonine to enable him to carry out the deed. Dionyza could be any age between late twenties and mid-forties.

Pericles is a play for which we have no authentic text and there is much dispute amongst academics on many of the details. The above is my own version based on five different editions.

I have cut lines of Marina, Leonine and Dionyza to construct this speech.

---

3   *With more than foreign heart.* As if I were a close relative.

5   *Our paragon to all reports* You who according to all reports (that he has received) is our very model of excellence

           thus blasted looking so ill

6   *breadth* length

8   *to your best courses* of what was the best for you

9   *Resume* (This is 'Reserve' in some editions.)

16   *softly* slowly

17   *What! I must have care of you.* Go on! I must make sure you do what's best for you. (There's a comma in place of the exclamation mark in some editions.)

Act 4, Scene 1 (Scene 15 in some versions)
Dionyza –

1   Come, come,
       I love the King your father and yourself
       With more than foreign heart. We every day
       Expect him here. When he shall come and find
5   Our paragon to all reports thus blasted,
       He will repent the breadth of his great voyage,
       Blame both my lord and me that we have taken
       No care to your best courses. Go, I pray you,
       Walk and be cheerful once again. Resume
10   That excellent complexion which did steal
       The eyes of young and old. Care not for me;
       I can go home alone.
       Come, come, I know 'tis good for you.
       [*to Leonine*] Walk half an hour, Leonine, at the least.
15   [*to Marina*] I'll leave you, my sweet lady, for a while.
       Pray walk softly, do not heat your blood.
17   What! I must have care of you.   *Exit Dionyza*

Pericles

The Bawd

The Bawd is the keeper of a brothel. At the beginning of this scene she complains, 'We were never so much out of creatures. We have but poor three, and they can do no more than they can do; and they with continual action are even as good as rotten'. Then a group of pirates arrive with the young Marina, the long-lost daughter of Pericles. The Bawd and her husband, Pandar, agree to buy Marina; and he leaves with the pirates to settle the finances, saying, 'Wife take her in; instruct her what she has to do, that she may not be raw in her entertainment'. The Bawd starts by commenting on Marina to her servant Boult. She could be any age above about mid-twenties.

I have constructed this speech from a number of shorter ones – imagining that Marina becomes silent, rather than protesting as she does in the play.

1	*take you the marks of her* look at the (feminine) assets she has
2	*warrant* guarantee
4	*maidenhead* virgin
6–7	*done their part in you.* (i.e. given you so much that's attractive to men.)
7	*are light* have fallen (by chance)
7–8	*are like to live.* will in all likelihood remain.
10	*the difference* a variety
	complexions types (of men)
	What Why
11	*Marry* Why, to be sure (a mild swear-word literally meaning, 'by the Virgin Mary')
	whip the gosling (i.e. confound the silly young creature; 'the' is 'thee' in some editions.)
12	*something to do* trouble
14	*must stir you up.* must rouse you. ('must' is not in some editions.)
17	*to* (This is not in some editions.)
20	*mere* clear

Act 4, Scene 2 (Scene 16 in some versions)
Bawd –

1   Boult, take you the marks of her, the colour of her hair,
     complexion, height, her age, with warrant of her virginity,
     and cry, 'He that will give most shall have her first'. Such a
     maidenhead were no cheap thing, if men were as they have
5   been. Get this done as I command you. [*Exit Boult*] Why
     lament you, pretty one? Come, the gods have done their part
     in you. You are light into my hands, where you are like to
     live. And you shall live in pleasure. Yes, indeed shall you,
     and taste gentlemen of all fashions. You shall fare well. You
10   shall have the difference of all complexions. What, do you
     stop your ears? Marry, whip the gosling! I think I shall have
     something to do with you. Come, you're a young foolish
     sapling, and must be bowed as I would have you. Men must
     comfort you, men must feed you, men must stir you up. Pray
15   you, come hither a while. You have fortunes coming upon
     you. Mark me: you must seem to do that fearfully which you
     commit willingly, to despise profit where you have most
     gain. To weep that you live as ye do makes pity in your
     lovers; seldom but that pity begets you a good opinion, and
20   that opinion a mere profit. Come your ways, follow me.

Richard II

Queen Isabel

Queen Isabel was the wife of King Richard II. In reality she was a child at the time of these events, however, Shakespeare gave her the maturity of someone at least in her early twenties. Although we see them only briefly together in the play, it seems to be a very loving relationship. In many ways she is the 'human interest' (in amongst all the politics) of the play.

Richard was one of those sometimes strong and good and sometimes weak and corrupt rulers – he was unlucky to be King at a time of economic crisis. At this point, Richard has not long gone on a military expedition to Ireland, whilst Isabel has been taken to safety at Berkeley Castle (just south of Gloucester) by the Duke of York, Richard's uncle. She has just overheard some gardeners talking about what's happened to Richard – news that was given to the Duke of York the night before, but which she only learns from what she's just overheard.

In the play, the Gardener responds between lines 9 and 10 with his apologies and sympathies, and with the observation that he spoke 'no more than everyone doth now'.

---

1   *pressed to death* (She is now bursting to speak after what she's heard. 'Pressing' was a punishment for those who refused to plead neither guilty or not guilty – heavy weights were placed on the accused's chest until they either pleaded or died.)

2   *old Adam's likeness* (Adam was the first gardener.)
       dress tend

4   *suggested* tempted

8   *Divine* Predict

11   *embassage* news (with the ironic undertone that it was given with all due formality by a diplomat from an embassy)

13   *serve me* serve (your message) on me

14   *Thy sorrow* The sorrow that you report

15   *London's king* (i.e. Richard, the true King.)

17   *triumph* (Isabel is thinking of the triumphal processions of victorious Roman armies, where prisoners played a prominent part in the display.)
       Bolingbroke (Richard's cousin, Henry Bolingbroke, who after Richard's deposition became King Henry IV.)

Act 3, Scene 4
Queen Isabel –

    The Duke of York's garden, Berkeley Castle
1   O, I am pressed to death through want of speaking!
    She comes forward
    Thou, old Adam's likeness, set to dress this garden,
    How dares thy harsh rude tongue sound this unpleasing news?
    What Eve, what serpent hath suggested thee
5   To make a second fall of cursèd man?
    Why dost thou say King Richard is deposed?
    Dar'st thou, thou little better thing than earth,
    Divine his downfall? Say where, when, and how
    Cam'st thou by this ill tidings? Speak, thou wretch.
10   Nimble mischance that art so light of foot,
    Doth not thy embassage belong to me,
    And am I last that knows it? O, thou think'st
    To serve me last, that I may longest keep
    Thy sorrow in my breast. Come, ladies, go
15   To meet, at London, London's king in woe.
    What, was I born to this – that my sad look
    Should grace the triumph of great Bolingbroke?
    Gard'ner, for telling me these news of woe,
19   Pray God the plants thou graft'st may never grow.
                         Exit with her Ladies

Richard III

The Duchess of York, Cicely Neville

The Duchess of York, Cicely Neville (1415–95) was the mother of
Richard III. He was the youngest of her four sons, the eldest being
Edward IV. She has just been comforting the son and daughter of her
other son, George, Duke of Clarence, who has recently died. Suddenly,
Queen Elizabeth (wife of Edward IV) enters 'with her hair about her
ears' and in her wailings tells them that Edward is also dead. This is
the Duchess' rejoinder. She was in her late sixties at the time, but could
be played younger.

Throughout the play she is a strong and sympathetic lady;
historically we know very little about her, but she did manage to live
until she was eighty (outliving Richard by ten years) – an incredible
achievement for those times.

1	*interest* right to share
2	*title* legal right
4	*images* (i.e. her sons: King Edward IV and George, Duke of Clarence.)
5	*mirrors* likenesses (i.e. her sons.)
14	*moiety* share
15	*overgo* exceed

Act 2, Scene 2
Duchess of York –

1   Ah, so much interest have I in thy sorrow
       As I had title in thy noble husband.
       I have bewept a worthy husband's death,
       And lived with looking on his images.
5   But now two mirrors of his princely semblance
       Are cracked in pieces by malignant death,
       And I for comfort have but one false glass
       That grieves me when I see my shame in him.
       Thou art a widow; yet thou art a mother,
10   And hast the comfort of thy children left.
       But death hath snatched my husband from mine arms
       And plucked two crutches from my feeble hands,
       Clarence and Edward. O, what cause have I,
       Thine being but a moiety of my moan,
15   To overgo thy woes and drown thy cries?

Richard III

Lady Anne

Lady Anne (Anne Neville, 1456–85) was the daughter of Warwick (a powerful member of the nobility and known as 'the king-maker') and married Richard of Gloucester (later King Richard III) in 1474. Shakespeare departs from history in (a) having her previously married (line 4) and (b) making Richard the murderer of both her (fictional) father-in-law (Henry VI) and her husband. (Historically they both died in 1471.) In the play we first see her at the funeral of Henry VI, where she curses Richard; but, he hypnotises her with his words and she agrees to marry him. This scene is twelve years later and Henry VI's successor, Edward IV, is not long dead; his son Edward V is only twelve and Richard is ruling the country as Lord Protector.

She is with Queen Elizabeth (Edward IV's widow), the Duchess of York (mother of Edward IV) and the Marquis of Dorset (Queen Elizabeth's son by her previous marriage). They are on their way to the Tower to see the young Edward V (and his brother). Firstly, they are barred from visiting the young princes and then she is suddenly summoned to Westminster 'to be crowned Richard's Queen'. The others make plans to escape Richard's evil, whilst Anne, 'with all unwillingness', decides to join him. Elizabeth has just said to her, 'wish thyself no harm'.

Her marvellous speeches in Act 1, Scene 2 are very popular audition fare.

2	*corse* corpse
4	*angel-husband* (Prince Edward, Henry VI's son. Not to be confused with the Edward who was Edward IV's son.)
5	*dear saint* (i.e. Henry VI.)
8	*so old a widow* (Historically, it is twelve years since the death of her first husband, Edward.)
15	*Grossly* Stupidly

Act 4, Scene 1
Lady Anne –

1 No? Why? When he that is my husband now
  Came to me as I followed Henry's corse,
  When scarce the blood was well washed from his hands,
  Which issued from my other angel-husband
5 And that dear saint which then I weeping followed –
  O when, I say, I looked on Richard's face,
  This was my wish: 'Be thou', quoth I, 'accursed
  For making me, so young, so old a widow,
  And when thou wed'st, let sorrow haunt thy bed;
10 And be thy wife – if any be so mad –
  More miserable by the life of thee
  Than thou hast made me by my dear lord's death.'
  Lo, ere I can repeat this curse again,
  Within so small a time, my woman's heart
15 Grossly grew captive to his honey words
  And proved the subject of mine own soul's curse,
  Which hitherto hath held mine eyes from rest;
  For never yet one hour in his bed
  Did I enjoy the golden dew of sleep,
20 But with his timorous dreams was still awaked.
  Besides, he hates me for my father Warwick,
22 And will, no doubt, shortly be rid of me.

The Tempest

Miranda

Miranda is the daughter of Prospero, the former Duke of Milan. Both were exiled when she was two and have lived for twelve years on the island where the play is set. Prospero has magic powers and has created the storm that is raging at this point, and which is threatening to destroy the ship that Miranda can see.

She is largely innocent of most of mankind's evils; everything she knows she has learned from her father, who is essentially a good, compassionate and loving human being. However, both are given to outbursts of anger – she is certainly not all sweetness and light when she confronts Caliban, Prospero's 'savage and deformed slave', who had once attempted to rape her.

Incidentally, her name – Latin for 'admirable' (literally, 'to be wondered at') – was invented by Shakespeare.

1	*art* magic
4	*welkin's* sky's
	cheek face
6	*brave* splendid
11	*or ere* before
13	*fraughting* cargo of (and 'those who are fraught', i.e. frightened)

Act 1, Scene 2
Miranda –

Enter Prospero and Miranda

1   If by your art, my dearest father, you have
Put the wild waters in this roar, allay them.
The sky, it seems, would pour down stinking pitch,
But that the sea, mounting to th' welkin's cheek,
5   Dashes the fire out. O, I have suffered
With those that I saw suffer! A brave vessel,
Who had, no doubt, some noble creature in her,
Dashed all to pieces! O, the cry did knock
Against my very heart! Poor souls, they perished.
10   Had I been any god of power, I would
Have sunk the sea within the earth, or ere
It should the good ship so have swallowed and
13   The fraughting souls within her.

The Tempest

Ariel

Ariel is a sprite or fairy – invisible to all but the magician Prospero, who rules the island (the setting of the play) and controls everybody and everything on it. Ariel's chief job is to carry out Prospero's wishes. At the beginning of the play she (or 'he' or 'it') contrived the wreck of the ship containing Prospero's enemies (Alonso, Sebastian, Antonio and others) whilst making sure that no-one was physically harmed. He leads the scattered survivors various merry dances round the island and not long before this speech Prospero arranges (magically) for a banquet to appear to the hungry men. They are just starting to eat when Ariel suddenly appears to them.

Ariel obviously enjoys his work – indeed, Prospero is very aware that in having all this fun Ariel might go too far in the heat of the moment. Ariel's moods go up and down quite violently – a bit like a child's. Ariel, the magical being, has very human feelings.

This is quite a long speech – you could start from, 'You fools! I and my fellows' (line 8).

Ariel can be played by either a man or a woman.

---

	harpy (A fierce, filthy and greedy monster; half woman and half bird.)
2	*That hath to instrument* That has for use (i.e. the power)
	this lower world (i.e. the Earth.)
3	*never-surfeited* always hungry
7	*such-like valour* the irrational courage of madness
8	*Their proper selves* Themselves
12	*still-closing waters* (waters which continually flow together again immediately after they've divided)
13	*dowle* small feather
14	*like* also
	could would
15	*massy* heavy
18	*From Milan did supplant* (Prospero was Duke of Milan before being ousted by these 'three'.)
19	*requit it* avenged (what they did to Prospero and, his daughter, Miranda)
25	*Ling'ring perdition* Slow ruin
27–30	*whose wraths... clear life ensuing* to escape the just retribution of these powers, repentance and a blameless future life is the only remedy. Otherwise, in this lonely place, they will have their revenge.
29	*is nothing but* there is no alternative but
30	*clear* blameless

Act 3, Scene 3
Ariel –

      Thunder and lightning. Ariel descends like a harpy, claps wings
      upon the table, and, with a quaint device, the banquet vanishes

1   You are three men of sin, whom Destiny –
      That hath to instrument this lower world
      And what is in 't – the never-surfeited sea
      Hath caused to belch up you; and on this island
5   Where man doth not inhabit, you 'mongst men
      Being most unfit to live. I have made you mad,
      And even with such-like valour men hang and drown
      Their proper selves.   [*Alonso, Sebastian, and Antonio draw*]
               You fools! I and my fellows
      Are ministers of Fate. The elements,
10   Of whom your swords are tempered may as well
      Wound the loud winds, or with bemocked-at stabs
      Kill the still-closing waters, as diminish
      One dowle that's in my plume. My fellow ministers
      Are like invulnerable. If you could hurt,
15   Your swords are now too massy for your strengths,
      And will not be uplifted.
           [*Alonso, Sebastian, and Antonio stand amazed*]
               But remember,
      For that's my business to you, that you three
      From Milan did supplant good Prospero;
      Exposed unto the sea, which hath requit it,
20   Him and his innocent child; for which foul deed,
      The powers, delaying not forgetting, have
      Incensed the seas and shores, yea, all the creatures,
      Against your peace. Thee of thy son, Alonso,
      They have bereft, and do pronounce by me
25   Ling'ring perdition – worse than any death
      Can be at once – shall step by step attend
      You and your ways; whose wraths to guard you from –
      Which here, in this most desolate isle, else falls
      Upon your heads – is nothing but heart's sorrow
30   And a clear life ensuing.   *Ascends and vanishes in thunder.*

Titus Andronicus

Tamora

Tamora, Queen of the Goths and her three sons have been captured by Titus, a Roman general and are brought to Rome. In a remarkably swift series of events one of her sons is sacrificed to appease the 'groaning shadows' of Titus' own sons killed in the war against the Goths; the remaining hostages are freed. Titus kills another of his sons over a matter of honour, and Saturninus, the new Emperor, declares his intention to marry Tamora. Meanwhile, Saturninus, fearful of Titus' popularity, picks a quarrel with him. Tamora, using her new status (seemingly) tries to rebuild relations between Saturninus and Titus. She starts off talking publicly, but makes her real intent clear in her aside to Saturninus – she wants revenge on Titus for the death of her own son, and this will be better done when the new Emperor's position is more secure. She could be as young as thirty.

1	*forfend* forbid
2	*be author* be the agent
3	*undertake* vouch
5	*Whose fury not dissembled speaks his griefs.* The fact that he is not able to disguise his anger shows the genuineness of his grievances. ('dissembled' = feigned)
7	*vain suppose* idle supposition
12	*patricians* the nobility
16	*at entreats* to entreaties
	let me alone leave it to me
18	*raze* destroy (This is 'race' in some editions, with the sense of 'root out'.)
24	*Take up* Bid him rise to his feet (and consequently bury your differences)
	good old man (i.e. Titus.)

Act 1, Scene 1
Tamora –

1   The gods of Rome forfend
       I should be author to dishonour you.
       But on mine honour dare I undertake
       For good lord Titus' innocence in all,
5   Whose fury not dissembled speaks his griefs.
       Then at my suit look graciously on him.
       Lose not so noble a friend on vain suppose,
       Nor with sour looks afflict his gentle heart.
       [*Aside to Saturninus*] My lord, be ruled by me, be won at last,
10   Dissemble all your griefs and discontents.
       You are but newly planted in your throne;
       Lest then the people, and patricians too,
       Upon a just survey take Titus' part,
       And so supplant you for ingratitude,
15   Which Rome reputes to be a heinous sin,
       Yield at entreats; and then let me alone:
       I'll find a day to massacre them all,
       And raze their faction and their family,
       The cruel father and his traitorous sons
20   To whom I sued for my dear son's life,
       And make them know what 'tis to let a queen
       Kneel in the streets and beg for grace in vain.
       [*Aloud*] Come, come, sweet Emperor; come, Andronicus,
       Take up this good old man, and cheer the heart
25   That dies in tempest of thy angry frown.

Titus Andronicus

Tamora

Tamora, Queen of the Goths was captured by Titus Andronicus, a Roman general and brought to Rome. She has three sons, the eldest of whom is sacrificed to appease the 'groaning shadows' of Titus' own sons killed in the war against the Goths. Rather soon after, Saturninus, the Roman Emperor, marries her and from this secure position Tamora begins to contemplate her revenge on Titus with the help of her lover, Aaron. She meets (at 'this place') Bassianus (brother to the Roman emperor) and his new wife Lavinia (daughter of Titus). Aaron also fetches her two remaining sons (Chiron and Demetrius) for her to tell them this incredible tale – which they swallow completely – in order to provoke them into taking revenge against Titus through Bassanius and Lavinia. At this point Tamora's sons have just arrived to find her with Bassanius and Lavinia, one says that she looks 'so pale and wan'. She could be as young as thirty.

In spite of the melodramatic language and situation, it is very important that her story is completely convincing.

2	*two* (i.e. Bassanius and Lavinia.)
	'ticed enticed
5	*Overcome* Choked
	baleful full of (active) evil
7	*fatal* foretelling death
8	*abhorrèd* loathsome
9	*dead time of the night* at the dead of night
11	*urchins* hedgehogs (These were generally associated with witchcraft or devils.)
14 & 16	*straight* immediately
17	*dismal yew* (Yew trees were associated with graveyards; their berries are poisonous, and some thought that the shadow of the tree would kill anyone sleeping under it.)

Act 2, Scene 3
Tamora –

1   Have I not reason, think you, to look pale?
       These two have 'ticed me hither to this place.
       A barren detested vale you see it is;
       The trees, though summer, yet forlorn and lean,
5   Overcome with moss and baleful mistletoe.
       Here never shines the sun, here nothing breeds
       Unless the nightly owl or fatal raven,
       And when they showed me this abhorrèd pit
       They told me here at dead time of the night
10   A thousand fiends, a thousand hissing snakes,
       Ten thousand swelling toads, as many urchins
       Would make such fearful and confusèd cries
       As any mortal body hearing it
       Should straight fall mad or else die suddenly.
15   No sooner had they told this hellish tale
       But straight they told me they would bind me here
       Unto the body of a dismal yew
       And leave me to this miserable death.
       And then they called me foul adulteress,
20   Lascivious Goth, and all the bitterest terms
       That ever ear did hear to such effect.
       And had you not by wondrous fortune come,
       This vengeance on me had they executed.
       Revenge it as you love your mother's life,
25   Or be ye not henceforward called my children.

Titus Andronicus

Lavinia

Lavinia is the daughter of Titus Andronicus, a Roman general, recently victorious over the Goths. He has returned to Rome with their Queen, Tamora and her three sons, the eldest of whom he sacrifices in order to appease the 'groaning shadows' of Titus' own sons killed in the war. Meanwhile, Saturninus, the Emperor, marries Tamora and from this secure position she begins to contemplate her revenge on Titus with the help of her lover, Aaron. Her first targets are Lavinia and her new husband Bassianus (the Emperor's younger bother), whom Tamora and her surviving sons (Demetrius and Chiron) encounter whilst out hunting. They kill Bassanius and then begin to threaten Lavinia. At first she pleads for her life, but then Tamora suggests that they 'satisfy their lust' on her. She could be any age between mid-teens and early twenties.

Chiron interrupts her final line and then he and his brother drag her off to rape and mutilate her. You could finish at line 15 or think of the final dash as an exclamation mark.

I have cut Demetrius' and Tamora's lines to construct this speech.

8	*present* immediate
9	*denies* forbids
15	*our general name* our (good) reputation as women
16	*Confusion fall* Destruction reign

Act 2, Scene 3
Lavinia –

1   O, let me teach thee for my father's sake,
       That gave thee life when well he might have slain thee.
       Be not obdurate, open thy deaf ears.
       [*Embracing Tamora's knees*]
       O Tamora, be called a gentle queen,
5   And with thine own hands kill me in this place;
       For 'tis not life that I have begged so long;
       Poor I was slain when Bassianus died.
       'Tis present death I beg, and one thing more
       That womanhood denies my tongue to tell.
10   O, keep me from their worse-than-killing lust,
       And tumble me into some loathsome pit
       Where never man's eye may behold my body.
       Do this, and be a charitable murderer.
       No grace, no womanhood – ah, beastly creature,
15   The blot and enemy to our general name!
16   Confusion fall –

Titus Andronicus

The Nurse

The Nurse is one of those intriguing characters who only has one scene in the whole play. The Empress she talks about is Tamora, Queen of the Goths who has married the Roman Emperor, Saturninus. Tamora also has a Moorish lover, Aaron, who is obviously the father of the baby. Tamora orders the Nurse to take the infant to Aaron. The Nurse has just found him with Tamora's two grown-up sons by a previous marriage: Demetrius and Chiron. We know nothing more about her and she could be any age you care to make her.

There is no denying the overt racism of this speech. This was normal in Shakespeare's time.

This speech is constructed from a scene of about one hundred lines. I have adapted one of Aaron's lines for her and cut a number of Aaron, Demetrius and Chiron's lines. I have also changed a few words.

1	*Good morrow* (This is 'God morrow' in some editions.)
8	*issue* child
10	*fair-faced* light-skinned
	clime country (literally: climate)
11	*thy stamp, thy seal* (She is acknowledging that he is the father.)
14	*'s* his

Act 4, Scene 2
Nurse –

Enter Nurse with a blackamoor child

1   Good morrow, lords.
      O, tell me, did you see Aaron the Moor?
      O gentle Aaron, we are all undone!
      Now help, or woe betide thee evermore!
5   Here, that which I would hide from heaven's eye,
      Our Empress' shame and stately Rome's disgrace.
      She is delivered, lords, she is delivered – a devil.
      A joyless, dismal, black, and sorrowful issue.
      Here is the babe, as loathsome as a toad
10   Amongst the fair-faced breeders of our clime.
      The Empress sends it thee, thy stamp, thy seal,
      And bids thee christen it with thy dagger's point.
      Aaron, you must; the mother wills it so
      Or the Emperor in 's rage will doom her death.
15   I say to you, no-one saw the child but
      Cornelia the midwife, and myself,
17   And no one else but the delivered Empress.

Troilus and Cressida

Cressida

Cressida is the daughter of a Trojan priest who has defected to the Greeks during the ten-year siege of Troy. She is secretly attracted to Troilus, a young Trojan prince, but as she says earlier, 'Things won are done; joy's soul lies in the doing'. Her uncle Pandarus is aware of her secret desires and pooh-poohs her equivocations and arranges for her to meet with Troilus – in this scene. To start with she and Troilus engage in the kind of verbal foreplay common to people desiring each other, but not quite able to commit themselves to love. Then Pandarus reappears and brings the conversation sharply back to sex. Suddenly she says openly to Troilus, 'I have loved you night and day / For many weary months' and shortly after, 'Stop my mouth' (i.e. 'Kiss me'), but then she shrinks away and almost leaves. Troilus then swears his eternal fidelity ending with, 'As true as Troilus' shall crown up the verse / And sanctify the numbers' ('numbers' = verses). This is her response.

5	*blind* unheeding
6	*characterless* without leaving a mark (hence, unrecorded)
	grated worn away
8	*false maids in love* maids who are false in love
12	*Pard* Leopard (or panther)
	hind female deer
	step-dame stepmother (proverbially unkind to her stepchildren)
13	*stick* pierce

Act 3, Scene 2
Cressida –

1   Prophet may you be!
       If I be false, or swerve a hair from truth,
       When time is old and hath forgot itself,
       When water-drops have worn the stones of Troy,
5   And blind oblivion swallowed cities up,
       And mighty states characterless are grated
       To dusty nothing – yet let memory,
       From false to false, among false maids in love,
       Upbraid my falsehood! When they've said, 'As false
10   As air, as water, wind or sandy earth,
       As fox to lamb, as wolf to heifer's calf,
       Pard to the hind, or step-dame to her son',
       Yea, let them say, to stick the heart of falsehood,
14   'As false as Cressid'.

Troilus and Cressida

Cressida

Cressida is the daughter of a Trojan priest who has defected to the Greeks during the ten-year siege of Troy. She is secretly attracted to Troilus, a young Trojan prince, but as she says earlier, 'Things won are done; joy's soul lies in the doing'. Her uncle Pandarus is aware of her secret desires and pooh-poohs her equivocations. He arranges for her to meet with Troilus, and after much hesitation they go to bed together. The following morning Pandarus returns to break the news to her that she is to be exchanged for a prisoner and must 'be gone from Troilus'.

In the play Pandarus has two short comments that break up this speech.

---

3   *touch of consanguinity* feeling of a blood relationship
7   *force* compulsion
14   *sounding* uttering

Act 4, Scene 2
Cressida –

1   O you immortal gods! I will not go.
      I will not, uncle. I have forgot my father;
      I know no touch of consanguinity;
      No kin, no love, no blood, no soul so near me
5   As the sweet Troilus. O you gods divine,
      Make Cressid's name the very crown of falsehood
      If ever she leave Troilus! Time, force, and death,
      Do to this body what extremes you can;
      But the strong base and building of my love
10   Is as the very centre of the earth,
      Drawing all things to it. I'll go in and weep,
      Tear my bright hair and scratch my praisèd cheeks,
      Crack my clear voice with sobs and break my heart
14   With sounding 'Troilus'. I will not go from Troy.

Exeunt

101

Troilus and Cressida

Cassandra

Cassandra is a prophetess and a princess of Troy during the pointless and interminable siege of that city. She is daughter of King Priam and sister of princes Hector, Troilus, and Paris. Earlier in the play she hysterically interrupts a council of war to warn of Troy's imminent destruction, only to be dismissed as the victim of 'brain-sick raptures'. Here she joins Andromache (Hector's wife) and Priam in trying to persuade Hector not to enter battle on a day of ill omens.

In Greek mythology her prophetic power was given to her by Apollo, but when she refused his love, he transformed it into a curse, causing her always to be disbelieved.

I have constructed this speech from a number of shorter ones and included four lines that are Andromache's in the play.

In the play (between lines 15 and 16) Hector and Troilus make it clear that they are going to go ahead with the battle. You could do this speech just down to line 15 or simply imagine that the men turn their backs and start to leave for the fight.

———————————

2	*notes of sally* trumpet-call (announcing that an army is about to go onto battle)
3	*peevish* headstrong
4	*abhorred* abhorrent
5	*spotted* tainted (In animal sacrifices to the gods, the entrails were examined, and a tainted liver was a signal of ill-omen.)
7	*To hurt by being just.* To fight (simply in order) to fulfil your vow.
8	*For we would give much* Because we would give generously
10	*purpose* rightness (of the cause)
11	*vows to every purpose must not hold.* not all vows should be held unbreakable.
13	*stay* support
15	*Fall all* All will fall
20	*dolours* griefs
22	*antics* grotesque clowns
24	*Yet* (This is 'Yes' in some editions.)
	soft wait and listen

Act 5, Scene 3
Cassandra –

> *Enter Cassandra*

1 Where is my brother Hector?
No notes of sally, for the heavens, sweet brother.
The gods are deaf to hot and peevish vows.
They are polluted off'rings, more abhorred
5 Than spotted livers in the sacrifice.
O, be persuaded. Do not count it holy
To hurt by being just. It is as lawful,
For we would give much, to use violent thefts,
And rob in the behalf of charity.
10 It is the purpose that makes strong the vow,
But vows to every purpose must not hold.
Unarm, sweet Hector; Priam, hold him fast.
He is thy crutch. Now if thou loose thy stay,
Thou on him leaning and all Troy on thee,
15 Fall all together. Priam, yield not to him!
O farewell, dear Hector!
Look how thou diest! Look how thy eye turns pale!
Look how thy wounds do bleed at many vents.
Hark how Troy roars; how Hecuba cries out;
20 How poor Andromache shrills her dolours forth.
Behold: distraction, frenzy, and amazement
Like witless antics one another meet,
And all cry, 'Hector, Hector's dead, O Hector!'
Farewell. Yet soft! Hector, I take my leave.
25 Thou dost thyself and all our Troy deceive.   *Exit*

Twelfth Night

Maria

Maria is a gentlewoman attending the Countess Olivia and a 'most excellent devil of wit'. She is great friends with Sir Toby Belch (Olivia's uncle) and his drinking companion, Sir Andrew Aguecheek. Sir Toby and Sir Andrew have just been chastised by Olivia's steward, Malvolio, for their rowdy, drunken behaviour. He also accuses Maria of giving 'means for this uncivil rule' and then flounces out. The trio are angry at Malvolio's treatment of them, then Maria contrives the following plot to embarrass him. She could be any age from late teens to early forties.

I have constructed this speeches from a number of shorter ones.

3	*let me alone with him.* leave him to me.
3–4	*gull him into a nayword* play such a trick on him to make him a byword ('nayword') for stupidity
4	*common recreation* laughing-stock
5	*I have wit enough to lie straight in my bed.* (i.e. the most instinctive and easiest thing in the world.)
7	*Puritan* (i.e. extremely precise and strict in moral and religious matters.)
7–8	*time-pleaser* self-seeking flatterer
8	*affectioned* affected
8–9	*cons state without book and utters it by great swathes* memorises expressions appropriate to high position and uses them profusely ('swathe' is 'swarths' or 'swarth' in some editions.)
9	*the best persuaded of himself* extremely self-conceited
11	*grounds of faith* firm belief
15	*expressure* expressive quality
16	*feelingly personated* vividly described
17–18	*on a forgotten matter we can hardly make distinction of our hands.* when neither of us remembers which of us wrote something, we cannot easily discover which it was from the writing.
19	*physic* medicine
20	*the fool* (This is Feste, Olivia's jester. Actually it is Fabian who makes the 'third' in Act 2, Scene 5.)
21	*construction* interpretation
22	*event* outcome

Act 2, Scene 3
Maria –

1   Sweet Sir Toby, be patient for tonight. Since the youth of the
Count's was today with my lady she is much out of quiet. For
Monsieur Malvolio, let me alone with him. If I do not gull
him into a nayword and make him a common recreation, do
5   not think I have wit enough to lie straight in my bed. I know
I can do it. Marry, sir, sometimes he is a kind of Puritan – the
devil a Puritan that he is, or anything constantly but a time-
pleaser; an affectioned ass that cons state without book and
utters it by great swathes; the best persuaded of himself, so
10   crammed, as he thinks, with excellencies, that it is his
grounds of faith that all that look on him love him – and on
that vice in him will my revenge find notable cause to work.
I will drop in his way some obscure epistles of love; wherein
by the colour of his beard, the shape of his leg, the manner of
15   his gait, the expressure of his eye, forehead, and complexion,
he shall find himself most feelingly personated. I can write
very like my lady your niece; on a forgotten matter we can
hardly make distinction of our hands. Sport royal, I warrant
you. I know my physic will work with him. I will plant you
20   two – and let the fool make a third – where he shall find the
letter. Observe his construction of it. For this night, to bed,
22   and dream on the event. Farewell.   *Exit*

Twelfth Night

Maria

Maria is a gentlewoman attending the Countess Olivia and a 'most excellent devil of wit'. She is great friends with Sir Toby Belch (Olivia's uncle) and his drinking companion, Sir Andrew Aguecheek. Maria, Sir Toby and Sir Andrew want revenge on Malvolio (Olivia's steward) for his pompous behaviour towards them. Maria has devised a plan whereby Malvolio discovers a letter (apparently from Olivia, but really forged by Maria) in which he is encouraged into various ridiculous actions to gain Olivia's love. Malvolio falls for the letter and Maria has just found Sir Toby and Sir Andrew to tell them of her success. She could be any age from late teens to early forties.

In the play Sir Toby has a short line in the middle; I have simply adapted it to fit Maria's flow.

1	*the spleen* a huge laugh (The spleen was supposed, amongst its other emotional functions, to be the source of uncontrollable laughter.)
2	*Yond gull* That fool over there ('Yond' implies that he is at some distance and is 'Yon' in some editions.)
3	*renegado* deserter from his faith
4–5	*such impossible passages of grossness* such obvious (and wildly improbable) statements (in Maria's letter)
6	*villainously* abominably
6–7	*pedant that keeps a school i' th' church* teacher who has to teach in the church (i.e. that he has no school-house of his own, which implies a certain poverty – not an image Malvolio would like.)
7	*murderer* (This is 'murtherer' in some editions.)
8	*betray* ensnare
9–10	*more lines than is in the new map with the augmentation of the Indies* (The new maps of the time were the first to contain what were then known as the 'East Indies' – now North and South America – and were covered with 'lines' of latitude and longitude.)
12	*take 't* (This is 'take it' in some editions. I prefer the shortened form as it reflects Maria's excitement.)

Act 3, Scene 2
Maria –

1   If you desire the spleen, and will laugh yourselves into
     stitches, follow me. Yond gull Malvolio is turned heathen, a
     very renegado; for there is no Christian, that means to be
     saved by believing rightly, can ever believe such impossible
5   passages of grossness. He's in yellow stockings and cross-
     gartered most villainously, like a pedant that keeps a school
     i' th' church. I have dogged him like his murderer. He does
     obey every point of the letter that I dropped to betray him. He
     does smile his face into more lines than is in the new map with
10   the augmentation of the Indies. You have not seen such a
     thing as 'tis. I can hardly forbear hurling things at him. I know
     my lady will strike him. If she do, he'll smile, and take 't for a
13   great favour.

The Two Gentlemen of Verona

Silvia

Silvia is the daughter of the Duke of Milan. She is in love with Valentine and loved by both Thurio and Proteus. (The latter has previously vowed his love to Julia.) She and Valentine plan to elope, but they are betrayed by Proteus to her father, who banishes Valentine. Proteus then starts to try to woo Silvia, but she spurns him. In this scene she has just appeared (at an upstairs window) and he tries again. This is her response.

I have edited two speeches together, adapted a line of Proteus' and cut an aside of Julia's, to construct this speech.

2	*presently* immediately
	hie hasten
3	*subtle* crafty
4	*conceitless* naïve
5	*To be* As to be
7	*make thy love amends* (i.e. to Julia.)
8	*pale queen of night* (i.e. the moon.)
17	*importunacy* importunity (i.e. your improper overtures toward me.)

Act 4, Scene 2
Silvia –

1   My will is even this,
       That presently you hie you home to bed.
       Thou subtle, perjured, false, disloyal man,
       Think'st thou I am so shallow, so conceitless
5   To be seducèd by thy flattery,
       That hast deceived so many with thy vows?
       Return, return, and make thy love amends.
       For me – by this pale queen of night I swear –
       I am so far from granting thy request
10   That I despise thee for thy wrongful suit;
       And by and by intend to chide myself
       Even for this time I spend in talking to thee.
       You say you did love a lady who is dead.
       Say that she be; yet Valentine, thy friend,
15   Survives, to whom, thyself art witness,
       I am betrothed. And art thou not ashamed
17   To wrong him with thy importunacy?

The Two Noble Kinsmen

The Second Queen

The Second Queen is one of three who suddenly appear to interrupt the wedding of Theseus (Duke of Athens) and Hippolyta (Queen of the Amazons). The Queens' husbands (their 'sovereigns') have been killed in an attack on Thebes. Creon (King of Thebes) ordered that their bodies should not be buried as a warning to others who might try the same thing. The first Queen has appealed to Theseus for revenge against Creon and he is very distressed at these events and needs time to think. She is followed by the second Queen who appeals to Hippolyta. We know nothing more about her, so she could be almost any age you like.

The idea of a body not being buried is repulsive to us, but at that time it also meant that the deceased's soul would wander eternally in torment.

2	*dreaded* deeply respected (and feared)
3	*scythe-tusked boar* (There are several stories in mythology about massive boars terrorising populations and being killed by assorted heroes and heroines.)
4	*wast near to make* was almost successful in making
6–7	*uphold creation in that honour / First Nature styled it in* ensure that everything continued to have the same degree of eminence which Nature gave to it at the creation (specifically, the primacy of man over woman)
8	*bound* proper limits (of womanly behaviour)
9	*force* power (as a soldier)
10	*equally* with justice
	poise balance
11	*on* over
12	*ow'st* possess (This is 'owest' in some editions.)
13–14	*is a servant for / The tenor of thy speech* will faithfully carry out your wishes (whatever they are)
14	*glass of ladies* model for womankind
17	*Require him* Ask of him that
18	*key* tone of voice (i.e. in distress, and so most likely to move Theseus.)
20	*Lend us a knee* Give us your support
22	*a dove's motion when the head's plucked off* (i.e. very briefly.)
23	*him* (i.e. Theseus.)
	blood-sized field battlefield covered with coagulated blood
23–4	*swoll'n, / Showing the sun his teeth, grinning at the moon* (i.e. as an unburied, rotting corpse.)

Act 1, Scene 1
Second Queen –

1   Honoured Hippolyta,
        Most dreaded Amazonian, that hast slain
        The scythe-tusked boar; that with thy arm, as strong
        As it is white, wast near to make the male
5   To thy sex captive, but that this thy lord,
        Born to uphold creation in that honour
        First Nature styled it in, shrunk thee into
        The bound thou wast o'erflowing, at once subduing
        Thy force and thy affection; soldieress,
10   That equally canst poise sternness with pity,
        Whom now I know hast much more power on him
        Than ever he had on thee, who ow'st his strength
        And his love too, who is a servant for
        The tenor of thy speech; dear glass of ladies,
15   Bid him that we, whom flaming war doth scorch,
        Under the shadow of his sword may cool us;
        Require him he advance it o'er our heads;
        Speak't in a woman's key – like such a woman
        As any of us three; weep ere you fail.
20   Lend us a knee;
        But touch the ground for us no longer time
        Than a dove's motion when the head's plucked off;
        Tell him if he i' th' blood-sized field lay swoll'n,
        Showing the sun his teeth, grinning at the moon,
25   What you would do.

The Two Noble Kinsmen

Hippolyta

Hippolyta is Queen of the Amazons, fiancée and later wife of Theseus, Duke of Athens. She is a strong, magnanimous and noble woman. She and Emilia, her sister, have just bidden farewell to Pirithous, a close friend of Theseus, to join the Duke in the war against Thebes. The women then get to talking about close-friendships between people of the same sex and this is Hippolyta's observations of the two men's relationship. She could be any age between mid-twenties and early forties.

The first two lines of this speech are adapted from a speech of Emilia's.

2	*labour* diligence
3	*cabined* sheltered together
5	*want* lack of necessities (food, etc.)
	contending (i.e. as to which was the severer hardship.)
	skiffed travelled in a small boat (a skiff)
7	*I' th' least of these* At their mildest
8	*where death's self was lodged* in the Underworld (In mythology, Theseus and Pirithous visited the Underworld in order to abduct Persephone, the wife of Hades, as a wife for Pirithous. Hades took them prisoner, but they were rescued by Hercules.)
9	*brought them off* rescued them
11	*so deep a cunning* such subtle skill
12	*outworn* worn out (by the passage of time, i.e. ended by death.)
15	*like* equal
	which he loves best (Hippolyta herself or his friend, Pirithous.)

Act 1, Scene 3
Hippolyta –

1   I have observed him,
        Since our great lord departed, with much labour;
        And I did love him for 't. They two have cabined
        In many as dangerous as poor a corner,
5   Peril and want contending; they have skiffed
        Torrents whose roaring tyranny and power
        I' th' least of these was dreadful, and they have
        Fought out together, where death's self was lodged;
        Yet fate hath brought them off. Their knot of love,
10   Tied, weaved, entangled, with so true, so long,
        And with a finger of so deep a cunning,
        May be outworn, never undone. I think
        Theseus cannot be umpire to himself,
        Cleaving his conscience into twain, and doing
15   Each side like justice, which he loves best.

The Two Noble Kinsmen

Hippolyta

Hippolyta is Queen of the Amazons, fiancée and later wife of Theseus, Duke of Athens. She is a strong, magnanimous and noble woman. She and Emilia, her sister, have just bidden farewell to Pirithous, a close friend of Theseus, to join the Duke in the war against Thebes. The women then get to talking about close-friendships between people of the same sex. Emilia has just talked at length about her childhood friendship with Flavinia, and finishes her speech with 'the true love 'tween maid and maid may be / More than in sex dividual.' This is Hippolyta's response. She could be any age between mid-twenties and early forties.

In the play Emilia has a short line between lines 4 and 5.

2	*high-speeded pace* rapid flow of words
10	*ripe for your persuasion* ready to be persuaded by you
14	*we* (i.e. herself.)

Act 1, Scene 3
Hippolyta –

1   You're out of breath,
        And this high-speeded pace is but to say
        That you shall never, like the maid Flavina,
        Love any that's called man.
5   Now alack, weak sister,
        I must no more believe thee in this point –
        Though in't I know thou dost believe thyself –
        Than I will trust a sickly appetite,
        That loathes even as it longs. But sure, my sister,
10   If I were ripe for your persuasion, you
        Have said enough to shake me from the arm
        Of the all-noble Theseus, for whose fortunes
        I will now in and kneel, with great assurance
        That we, more than his Pirithous, possess
15   The high throne in his heart.

The Two Noble Kinsmen

Emilia

Emilia is the sister of Hippolyta (Queen of the Amazons, fiancée and later the wife of the Duke of Athens, Theseus). Almost certainly this speech is Shakespeare's but because parts of the play were probably written by John Fletcher she is a somewhat confusing character. However, she is certainly a warm-hearted, sensitive young woman. The 'kinsmen' (Arcite and Palamon) are both in love with Emilia, and after several quarrels, Theseus agrees to arrange a duel to decide who shall have her in marriage. This is about to start; Theseus and Hippolyta have been trying to persuade Emilia to watch but she can't face it. They leave her on her own and these are her thoughts as she awaits the outcome.

1	*gently visaged* appears gentle
2	*an engine bent* a weapon (e.g. bow or catapult) tensioned (and therefore ready for action)
3	*In a soft sheath* (i.e. safely cushioned.)
5	*aspect* appearance
6	*graved* furrowed (and a pun on graves)
7	*to* with
8	*quality* nature
9	*object* objective
10	*Becomes him nobly* Suits him well
13	*humours* moods
14	*Stick misbecomingly* Look unattractive
15	*Live in fair dwelling* Are becoming
16	*spirit* courage
17	*proof* trial by combat
19	*spoiling of his figure* mutilation of his body
20	*Enough* Would be sufficient
	chance misfortune
23	*forfeit an offence* miss an opportunity for attack
24	*craved that very time* needed to be taken immediately

Act 5, Scene 3
Emilia –

Emilia takes out two pictures, which she holds, one in each hand.

1   Arcite is gently visaged, yet his eye
Is like an engine bent, or a sharp weapon
In a soft sheath; mercy and manly courage
Are bedfellows in his visage. Palamon
5   Has a most menacing aspect; his brow
Is graved and seems to bury what it frowns on;
Yet sometime 'tis not so, but alters to
The quality of his thoughts. Long time his eye
Will dwell upon his object. Melancholy
10   Becomes him nobly; so does Arcite's mirth;
But Palamon's sadness is a kind of mirth,
So mingled, as if mirth did make him sad,
And sadness merry. Those darker humours that
Stick misbecomingly on others, on him
15   Live in fair dwelling.
[*Cornets. Trumpets sound as to a charge*]
Hark, how yon spurs to spirit do incite
The princes to their proof! Arcite may win me,
And yet may Palamon wound Arcite to
The spoiling of his figure. O, what pity
20   Enough for such a chance? If I were by,
I might do hurt, for they would glance their eyes
Toward my seat, and in that motion might
Omit a ward or forfeit an offence
Which craved that very time. It is much better
25   I am not there – O better never born
26   Than minister to such harm!

The Winter's Tale

Perdita

Perdita is the long-lost daughter of King Leontes and Queen Hermione of Sicilia – not that she knows any of this until the very end of the play; she has been brought up by a simple shepherd. She is a straight-forward and charming young girl in love with Florizel, son of the King of Bohemia. At this point she has just arrived with Florizel for the shepherds' festival. He has just complimented her on her costume, comparing her to a 'Queen'; this is her response. She is sixteen.

I have edited three of her speeches together to construct this speech.

2	*extremes* extravagances (in his costume)
4	*mark o' th' land* object of everyone's attention
5	*wearing* costume
6	*pranked up* dressed up showily
	But that Were it not that
7	*mess* group (of people)
	folly (i.e. people who behave foolishly.)
	feeders (i.e. the others eating at the feast.)
8	*Digest it with a custom* Put up with it because they have become accustomed to it. ('a custom' is 'accustom' in some editions.)
9	*swoon* (This is 'sworn' in some editions.)
10	*show myself a glass.* if I were to see myself in a mirror.
11	*difference* (i.e. in rank or status between us.)
16	*Vilely* Wretchedly (This is 'Vildly' in some editions.)
	bound up dressed
17	*flaunts* showy costume
21	*these two* (i.e. 'that you must change this purpose, or I my life'.)
23	*Or I my life.* (i.e. for the worse.)

Act 4, Scene 4
Perdita –

> *Enter Florizel dressed as Doricles a countryman, and Perdita as*
> *Queen of the Feast*

1   Sir, my gracious lord,
To chide at your extremes it not becomes me –
O, pardon that I name them! Your high self,
The gracious mark o' th' land, you have obscured
5   With a swain's wearing; and me, poor lowly maid,
Most goddess-like pranked up. But that our feasts
In every mess have folly, and the feeders
Digest it with a custom, I should blush
To see you so attired – swoon, I think,
10   To show myself a glass.
To me the difference forges dread; your greatness
Hath not been used to fear. Even now I tremble
To think your father, by some accident,
Should pass this way, as you did. O, the Fates!
15   How would he look to see his work, so noble,
Vilely bound up? What would he say? Or how
Should I, in these my borrowed flaunts, behold
The sternness of his presence? O, but sir,
Your resolution cannot hold when 'tis
20   Opposed, as it must be, by th' power of the King.
One of these two must be necessities,
Which then will speak that you must change this purpose,
23   Or I my life.

Bibliography

The Plays

I referred to the Arden, New Penguin, Oxford, Peter Alexander and Riverside editions and found different aspects to recommend each of them. If I'm to recommend one particular edition – for actors – I would marginally recommend the Oxford editions. *The Complete Works* were published in 1988 by Oxford University Press, and about half of the individual plays have appeared in paperback with some excellent notes. The remaining plays are 'forthcoming'.

Shakespeare Reference

Charles Boyce, *Shakespeare – The Essential Reference to His Plays, His Poems, His Life, And More* (Roundtable Press).
Peter Quennell and Hamish Johnson, *Who's Who in Shakespeare* (Routledge, 1996).

About Shakespeare and His Plays

There are an impossible number of books on this subject; the ones I've got most out of are:
Anthony Burgess, *Shakespeare* (Penguin, 1970) – this not a history book but a wonderful evocation of who Shakespeare might have been and how he might had lived his life.
A. L. Rowse, *Shakespeare the Elizabethan* (Weidenfeld & Nicholson, 1977) – although written by an eminent academic historian, this is a good read.
Jan Kott, *Shakespeare Our Contemporary* (1964) – although he writes about only a few of the plays, the author gives a wonderful evocation of Shakespeare in our time.

About Acting and Auditioning

Uta Hagen, *A Challenge for the Actor* (Macmillan, 1991) – the best book on acting ever written.
Simon Dunmore, *An Actor's Guide to Getting Work* (A & C Black, 1996) – all you need to know about auditioning and all aspects of being an actor.
Simon Dunmore, *Alternative Shakespeare Auditions for Women* (A & C Black, 1997) – my first collection of fifty speeches.
Ellis Jones, *Teach Yourself Acting* (Hodder & Stoughton Ltd., 1998) – a good overview of acting and the profession.